Cry to be Heard!

My Road to Recovery

To William Foyster
my paternal Grandfather
who gave me so much inspiration

Cry to be Heard!
My Road to Recovery

Steven Foyster

PAUL DICKSON BOOKS

Cry to be Heard!

Cry to be Heard! Published by Paul Dickson Books, September 2021

Paul Dickson Books, 156 Southwell Road, Norwich NR1 3RP
t. 01603 666011, **e.** paul@pauldicksonbooks.co.uk,
www.pauldicksonbooks.co.uk

ISBN
Paperback 978-1-9160550-7-0
E-book   978-1-9160550-8-7

A CIP catalogue record for this book is available from the British Library

Text and cover design: Brendan Rallison

Steven Foyster cover phototograph © Norfolk and Suffolk NHS Foundation Trust

Printed by Interprint in Norwich

Contents

Photographs between pages 67 and 70

Steve's paternal Grandmother and Grandfather, Ethel and William Foyster

Steve's parents, Roy and Doreen Foyster

The pond at the old Norfolk and Norwich Hospital visited by Steve on a memorable early outing in a wheelchair (see p.42). Photograph, Paul Dickson

Mundesley Hospital, photograph David Baker Photography

Foreword

Most of this intensely moving and thought-provoking book focuses on a relatively short period which began thirty-five years ago. Its content is, however, of searing contemporary importance. We are living at a time of almost unprecedented strangeness and uncertainty as, on a global scale, humanity does battle with a lethal virus which bears comparison with some of the deadliest plagues that have ravaged the earth in past centuries.

It is a time when millions of people are asking themselves profound existential questions about the meaning of life and about the significance of their own existence in particular. For many – and especially, it would seem, for depressed and disoriented young men – answers to these questions are often bleak in the extreme and, in deep despair, many choose to end their lives before they have even truly begun.

It was in such despair that Steve Foyster chose with passionate intent to seek oblivion one sunny May day in 1986. The mode of his intended exit from this world was dramatic and it perhaps warrants the word 'miraculous' that he did not succeed. Nonetheless, the multiple injuries he sustained on that fateful day have impacted on the whole of his life and day by day his body with its impairment and its amazing resilience, reminds him of the history of his journey from despair to hope, from apparent meaninglessness to profound purpose, from a sense of deep alienation to an experience of the warm embrace of the cosmos and of the unconditional acceptance of an ever-loving God.

The book tells the story of Steve's gradual recovery from his horrific injuries to the point where – against all the odds – he could walk again, resume employment, find a new partner and start a family. Along the way, he meets many remarkable people, many of them doctors, nurses, physiotherapists and care-workers who never abandoned faith in him and bestowed upon him a measure of professional skill and loving attentiveness which is at times breath-taking. I am constantly reminded of the remarkable accounts we read today of the devotion to duty and the unswerving vocational commitment of those who care for Covid patients whose lives depend upon such selfless labour. Nothing could illustrate more vividly our interdependence as a human family and how gloriously we can embrace our membership one of another when nothing less will do.

As Steve gradually recovers, it would seem that God, always somehow present in the shadows, becomes more manifest. Through friends, clergy, choirs, liturgies, books and other hidden ways God finds a way into Steve's inmost being and takes up residence. It is perhaps this inexorable process of the divine indwelling which makes 'Cry to be Heard' such an inspirational read. I believe, too, that it is a chuckling God who enables Steve to write with such panache and with such an irresistible sense of humour. His directness, his wry observations on some of the absurdities of human behaviour, his uncontainable mirth, thread their way through what is often a harrowing narrative and turn it into an enjoyable page-turner.

All of life is here – and that includes death and eternity – so that contradictions become tenable paradoxes and darkness gives way to light. It would seem unlikely material but I commend this book on pain, suffering and attempted self-destruction as a source not only of hope beyond despair but also of unexpected merriment. It may well make you weep but it will also make you smile or even laugh out loud.

Brian Thorne
Emeritus Professor, University of East Anglia and Co-founder
of the Norwich Centre.
Norwich, March 2021.

Introduction

This is a recovery story but only covers four years of my life in relative detail. Yet our recovery from any trauma, whether mental, physical, loss or abusive is ongoing until our last breath of our mortal life.

I wrote most of the first fifteen chapters which comprise the first two parts in longhand italics completely from memory, during the spring of 1987 which I found very cathartic. I had kept no diary or journal. I added in some medical and nursing notes having bought a set from my local hospital trust in 2019 and found to my delight that the time frames and the description of my condition that I had recalled from my' little grey cells' proved very accurate.

I have also included some reflections that I have made over the past few years. The third part was brought together during the past year using letters I have kept since 1986, medical notes and various other official correspondence.

I hope that it gives some insight, provokes some thought and even makes you laugh, surely one of the most precious gifts we have been given to share. This story is dedicated especially to my family, but also to many nursing professionals, friends and colleagues who have given so much to me along the long and winding road …

Steven Foyster
Norwich, February 2021

Part One

It's not the despair; It's the hope

Chapter 1
Close To The Edge

A spider takes its first web-creating leap. Are there no lengths to which it will go to produce its homespun masterpiece? The bejewelled finished article looks so perfect, such a safe haven. Yet one ill-met snag and the whole of the spider's world falls apart.

My paternal grandmother was very special to me, as grandparents often are. She became even more precious to me after the death of her beloved husband Billy. I saw him bear the severe pain brought on by a trapped cervical nerve, with such tenacity and frustration during the last seven years of his mortal life. He should have been enjoying the freedom of retirement from decades of labouring in the 'hell-holes' of shoe factories, as he described them.

I vividly remember him endeavouring to join in a game at a family trip to the beach, surrounded by his three children, their spouses and five grandchildren. He was very unwell. Most of us realised that it would probably be a farewell summer gathering and we subsequently were falsely jolly. Yet despite the obvious pain behind Billy's eyes, he still attempted to head the ball. His actions and words continue to inspire me 40 years after he passed on out of agony.

Ever since I was a small child, I saw my grandmother at least once a week. She was a bit like a bountiful goddess, ever constant, giving, giving, always giving; anything from sweets, to time, to assurance, but never really advice.

She asked for nothing in return except love, the love of her family. One of my all-time achievements was to leave her flat not only empty-handed but also after giving her something, a piece of fruit.

Maybe that was the first time that I realised it is just as important to receive as to give. I have had to take and receive a lot in the past 30 years, initially with a great imbalance in the amount of giving, or so I perceived it. It is important to receive with good grace, and by doing so, you are often unaware of what you might be giving back.

I have found it a great consolation that Jesus took everything good he was offered; food, wine, a bed for the night, the caress of a woman's hair on his feet, anointing perfume, a tomb from a wealthy follower.

My grandmother accepted me without condition, once openly stating that she would love me even as a murderer. I believed her. However, unlike Christ in the temple, I never witnessed a righteous anger. I know that other family members did see an angry, aggressive side to Ethel, as senility took hold in her last year.

Whenever anything good happened for several years after she died, I still wanted to call her with the news. I think when you love someone all your life you want to believe they are immortal.

From when I was four my parents went to the 'pictures' every other week. Cinemas still spattered the city centre, with huge single screens. Every fortnight my mother would meet my father outside City Hall. Working for the City Council architect's department he had alternate Thursday afternoons and Saturday mornings off.

Those afternoons often found me on long halcyon traipses with 'nanny' around our council estate, leading onto Mousehold Heath, or through wild-flowered fields, which have long succumbed to outdated tower blocks and a high school, (or I should I now say academy).

Returning from one such jaunt, we came across a local authority workman, painstakingly tamping down the edges of a freshly concreted footpath.

'Don't let that young'un spoil my cement' he admonished, half-jokingly.

'Oh, he would not dream of doing a thing like that' came my grandmother's instant retort. 'He is not that sort of boy.'

I spent the next quarter of a century trying to live up to and live down that reputation.

It was a sunny February lunchtime in 1986. I found myself standing, quite precariously on the parapet of Rose Lane multi-storey car park in the centre of Norwich, my toes edging towards the drop. I had been severely depressed for over a year, caused, I believed, by being emotionally and mentally drained in several directions.

During the previous year my wife had been suffering from a severe bout of ulcerative colitis, losing so much weight that in the end I had to carry her to the bathroom. I held it all in, as she did not want her parents to know. The family run business that I had put heart and soul into was moving in a downward financial spiral and, after my wife recovered, we had a major prostate cancer scare with her elderly father.

I felt that I was being somehow squeezed into a function rather than the person that I used to recognise. I felt totally numb, no longer had the capacity to love anyone, least of all myself. I also thought that I was going mad. Looking back, I think I was in fact insane, if you take that to mean 'out of my normal mind'.

I was desperately trying to hold down a temporary job after being let go from my previous employment because of my illness. Nearly seven years of extreme loyalty and dedication was wiped out by a mental, rather than physical weakness. I did not have the confidence to question the unfairness. I was an incomplete and utter emotional wreck.

Considering my mental state, remarkably I had applied for more than 30 jobs within three months, attended half a dozen interviews and finally acquired a definite post. Nevertheless this 'success' did not fill the loss of personal identity within a role I had truly loved, as well as the friendship of colleagues, reps and customers.

I edged even closer to the brink. 'Oh let's just do it!' I thundered inside, really quite worn out with the prevarication. Throughout the previous months I had developed uncharacteristic mood swings, becoming fairly violent at times, punching lampposts, both to injure myself through self-loathing and ultimately to hopefully gain sympathy from visible injuries.

On one occasion I smashed a fist sized hole through a substantial partition wall in our bathroom. My first wife obviously found these episodes extremely upsetting and threatening, not least because it was so different to my 'normal' behaviour.

I was on a course of antidepressants, the first thing a GP had hurled at me. He had also referred me to a private psychiatrist friend of his, as the NHS referral wait was quite long.

Unfortunately I found this man to be completely insensitive, arrogant and chauvinistic. He kept we waiting for 15-20 minutes prior to the commencement of each session, which would make me even more nervous and still charged me an arm and a leg. I have since heard that he had a notoriously poor reputation, so at least my intuition had stayed intact, even though it gave me no solace at the time.

My toes were now overlapping the parapet. There was no reason and no need to exist; tomorrow would be just the same, and the next day, and the next ... a black mist shrouded my shrivelled soul. Still I hesitated. It looked a long way down. Suddenly a woman and two girls, possibly her daughters, entered the car park directly below me, idly chattering and laughing. How dare they feel so happy?

Well good old Steve had better wait. He would not want to make too much mess on the concrete, now would he? After all, he is not supposed to be 'that sort of boy'.

A man was also watching me quite intensely from his car, parked about 20 metres away. I was half hoping that he would just disappear and let me do it. Do it, do it, do it. Give me no choice.

Yet there was something pulling me back, possibly him, possibly naked fear. After an eternity, which was probably only a couple of minutes, the man emerged from his spacious white saloon and beckoned me off the wall and into the other world of his Jaguar's upholstery.

His name was Bob and he worked for a regional television company.

'Whatever is the matter?' he asked, seemingly genuinely concerned.

I began to spill out my woes, swiftly dissolving into tears. I started to get rather angry at some of his sympathetic replies.

After patiently listening to what must have sounded like a load of incoherent garbage, Bob promptly decided to take the afternoon off work and whisked me to his home for a chat.

A mixture of emotions swirled to the surface. I was amazed at the reaction of this complete stranger. I was relieved that I had some concrete company rather than the company of concrete, dubious that anyone could help me and guilty to inconvenience the good Samaritan.

After all, I started to convince myself, having expressed how terrible I felt compared to the rest of humankind, that there was no need to pursue the matter any further. This was getting out of proportion. I was just a fraud, that's all, a sick fraud.

A few minutes into the journey, we paused at a red light and Bob turned to me and said, 'You know what the answer to all your problems is?'

'No' I replied bluntly, perusing a full-frontal lobotomy or a bullet through the brain.

'God', he announced, somewhat triumphantly.

It was just as well the lights changed or I would have been out of the car door.

I do not think I actually replied. My brain was in overdrive.

'Oh no! A religious weirdo. I am going to be abducted and brainwashed by a strange sect. Or maybe we are about to enter the do-goody Christian routine; tea, slightly damp biscuits, with a slice of St Paul on the side. Well you can disappear to your sanctimonious haven Bob. And you can let me out now.'

I did not say any of this. I do not know why. Possibly because Bob seemed so normal. Possibly because I was too tired to resist.

We arrived at my guardian angel's spacious yet unpretentious rural abode. I was introduced to Bob's equally normal wife, Ann, who did not seem the least bit phased by my arrival. 'Must happen everyday,' I thought.

I was given coffee and firm biscuits. St Paul was thankfully off the menu. There were two lively and loveable dogs, and later I was introduced to their equally lively teenage children. Maybe these people were OK. Perhaps Bob had not said God, but cod. After all fish was supposed to be good for the brain.

God, Jesus and Christianity were seldom, if ever, mentioned in our childhood home. My mother was extremely suspicious of the church, seeing it as totally hypocritical. Her father once told a suspected tract distributor to go away in no uncertain terms, only to discover he had come to read the meter. Her mother, who was deeply suspicious to the extent of keeping scuttle loads of coal in her wardrobe for good luck, may well have had an influence on her. As a teenager, I remember being warned by my mother not to use the church as a crutch.

Nevertheless, from an early age I prayed religiously for long lists of people, kneeling beside my light blue candlewick bedspread, never prompted to do so by anyone. This rigid habit, which became quite obsessive, finally lapsed halfway through junior school. In R.E. lessons I became fascinated by the Gospel stories and still have my version of the 'big catch' stored away in my momento box, written when I was about nine.

At grammar school I avoided the Christian Union like the mould ridden outside lavatories. It clashed with 15-a-side soccer scrimmages at lunchtime. I noticed rather smugly that most of the CU-ites were not very good at soccer.

When I did go to Methodist youth group meetings on a couple of occasions, my motives were hardly devout. I was a lonely adolescent, hormonally desperate for female company and there was a good darts board. I made only one new friend called Claude, no doubt due to my unwillingness to participate.

I discovered that nearly all the girls had been requisitioned by various pubescent saints who relied on biblical quotations as foreplay. I soon faded away, missing only the darts board and Claude's mad sense of humour.

At 17, the death of Billy severely tested my belief in any loving omnipresence. He died of bronchial pneumonia on the same day as my clarinet teacher, Mr Unwin, of whom I was also rather fond. Well if there is an omniscient God I railed, he must be a bit of a nasty bastard.

In 1980 I married Sue, a not very strict Roman Catholic and thus suffered a boring half-decipherable mass, in a cold barren cathedral once a week for my sins, which must have been manifold. Sue regarded me as waivering between agnostic and atheist, which was fairly astute.

I had not ever 'gone to church' before I married, apart from the occasional wedding, which after all is not a 'proper' service. I never even attended Billy's funeral, which I still regret. My parents thought it would be too upsetting for me, which was a great shame. If you are not allowed to get upset at funerals, then when are you? It is difficult to get through the grieving process when you are not even allowed to start.

My introduction to formalised worship via incense swinging, some Latin texts and dozens of respectable citizens unhygienically kissing a pair of marble feet every Good Friday, was possibly not ideal. It also served to enforce my mother's doctrine that the church is manipulative and not to be trusted.

In our pre-nuptual get to know the priest session, I blatantly asked the well-meaning canon how the regular members of the congregation could put up with the dry, monotonous ritual. I cannot recall receiving an adequate reply, but strangely I thought, some silent empathy.

Bob and Ann seemed to put a new light on things. We chatted for most of the afternoon. They did not pressurise or judge. Ann shared her fight against a tumour, which although not cured, was at least in remission. Even in that brief time I glimpsed the tenacity of her faith. Maybe some echoes of Billy resounded. He had read the Bible twice, but never discussed it with me.

Bob then threw in something I was none too keen about. He and Ann were both due to attend a Full Gospel Businessmen's supper that evening. They wanted me to go as well. What exactly was a Full Gospel Businessman? Someone who got second helpings?

There was always a hook to these evangelists I pondered, somewhat bitterly. However, rather than be rude and refuse, I decided to hedge my bets. I suggested to Bob that he should ring my wife. If she was amenable, then we would both go.

Bob went to the telephone, returning with a triumphant smile. My heart sank. He had explained to Sue that he had met me in rather unusual circumstances, but that I was OK. My wife was willing to go.

After almost a year of constant emotional drain, I think she would have considered virtually anything. We had even toyed with the idea of hypnotherapy, but I had been advised that this would have conflicted with the wonderful psychiatric treatment. Bob rang the organiser. His beam would have outdone the Cheshire Cat's. There were only two tickets left.

When we arrived at the hall I felt even more out of my depth. It was bursting at the seams with smartly dressed, mainly middle-aged men with add-on wives, who occasionally embraced each other like long lost souls. I wanted out, but in my hesitation to feign an apoplectic fit, we were guided to our table. The food was fine. Fish amazingly, so cod was indeed with us.

After the repast there was hearty singing of short, very repetitive, bits of music called choruses. People then started standing up and telling everybody something personal about themselves. I just could not relate to this crowd of grown men and women shouting out 'Praise the Lord' and bursting forth with examples of divine-personal relationships, telling the world how Jesus Christ had entered their lives that very week, that very hour, that very nanosecond.

For goodness sake, these people were English. Where was the sense of restraint? Had year upon year of failure at all national sports taught them nothing about the gift of subdued optimism?

Suddenly in the midst of all the hubbub, a goliath of a clergyman stood up to address the assembled multitude. Things simmered down. I cannot remember a word he said, or for how long he spoke, yet somehow I felt drawn to this man, by his very stature, his sincerity, his calmness and his conviction.

Using the current ecclesiastical vernacular he was charismatic, yet in the best possible taste. This huge clergyman announced that there was someone in the room who was deeply disturbed. Would he or she come forward for laying on of hands? I was sceptically stunned. Had Bob or Ann tipped him off? Not the case, I later discovered. Was this man psychic? Or perhaps everybody in the room was always emotionally disturbed at these soirées. I definitely did not want to partake in this faith healing mumbo jumbo, however well-meaning it might be.

No-one was moving. Then somehow I felt I was in someone else's body as I stood up and stumbled past empty chairs, seemingly willed by something devoid of logic or embarrassment towards this gentle giant. Sue was by my side. He asked me my name and simply said a short prayer, before laying his huge goalkeeper sized hands on my head. I felt some sort of release.

By the time we returned to our table both my wife and I were sobbing.

Bob and Ann were also in tears. 'Everything will be all right now', they reassured us.

In fact everything got much worse, but I still believe that when Reverend David Broome took my anguish in his large, tender hands, I was held safe.

Chapter 2
Too Late To Save Myself?

The situation deteriorated, even though Bob and Ann and several other friends were amazingly supportive. I went to one of my newfound friends' church praise worship services and even attended bible study. I felt really out of my depth. Everything seemed so easy to solve in the never-ending sermons, when the last point was made at least three times. But then it was back to my bleak reality when I walked out of the church door.

Bob invited me to do some filming and editing at his private studio, where he produced Christian themed videos. This offer filled me with abject terror, not the involvement but the responsibility of attending and maybe getting it 'wrong'. I stayed in bed until an hour before I was due to drive the 25 miles.

We did the filming and I actually found the editing fascinating. The final product could be completely altered from the original; a bit like my facade and the reality behind it. Yet any fragile confidence gained in participating was being quickly eroded, as the ebb tide of fear encroached to such an extent that a cliff slide seemed inevitable.

I had to relinquish a temporary job that was filling some time before I commenced a new permanent one at the beginning of April. Depression deepened, suicidal thoughts became so real that my wife farmed me off to my parents, for safety's sake; her's or mine, or both?

I should not have blamed her for abandoning me. I did. I was not interested in the problems that she was encountering, especially at work, due to the outside pressures caused by yours truly. I was not interested in ANYBODY else's problems. I had been so good at helping EVERYONE else out of the damaged concrete, now it was their turn.

I reacted with anger to my exile.

One morning I swallowed a dozen antidepressants, told my parents and was immediately whisked off to casualty, where I suffered the ignominy of having my stomach pumped, possibly the worst physical experience I hade ever had. Would-be overdosers beware.

It is simply horrific having a half inch rubber tube rammed down into your stomach without any anaesthetic, while all your body wants to do is gag it up. Nevertheless I had achieved my evil intention by dragging Sue away from her work place.

For the next month I oscillated between my parents' house and my 'home', depending on how much my wife trusted me. If I was behaving like a 'naughty child' I was banished to my childhood environment. If I behaved more like a 'responsible adult' I was allowed back to the jointly mortgaged abode, maybe for a couple of nights.

I inflicted cruel deeds or tricks to gain revengeful attention. On one occasion, waiting for Sue to return quite late at night, I pretended to be unconscious by not reacting to her arrival, much to her shock and concern.

Everything came to a head on the morning of March 21. During a bitter row, I endeavoured to force some antidepressants down my wife's throat, in an effort to calm her down.

Having understandably been met with some resistance, I shot a few down my own throat for good measure. Although I knew I had only swallowed a small number, Sue unsurprisingly did not believe me and dialled the emergency services.

Within minutes I was in an ambulance, about to endure an experience I had vowed that I would never, ever let myself face again. It was made doubly worse as this time I knew the width of that tube.

As this rigmarole was becoming somewhat tedious for the staff at A & E, the medical powers that be decided to my great relief and no doubt my wife's, to section me under the Mental Health Act.

Now we would really get to the root of the problem. I had all my clothes taken away apart from my socks and briefs, and was issued with regulation pyjamas and dressing gown. My parents brought in my comforting leather slippers. I was shown to my own narrow bed, with my own chipped bedside cabinet, in a drab, barren ward, smelling of disinfectant and despair.

I shared the ward with three other males aged between 20 and 60. It was still a comfort to be there. I was in a world of my own in a little part of the universe where the harsh reality of life could not, at least for a while, claw away at my soul.

I was given a complete check by a very pleasant doctor who questioned me about my medical well-being, or rather lack of it. I thought he seemed unduly preoccupied with the possibility that I heard voices telling me to do things. I had not the faintest idea what he was on about.

However, I soon witnessed some horrific results of this phenomenon, when a patient stabbed himself in the stomach, evidently brought on by demonic demands.

I remained at the clinic for nine days, a ridiculously short time to get to the root of anything, let alone 'grasp the nettle'. Of course I did not really want to grasp the nettle. Perversely, now that I had arrived in hospital, I wanted to get out.

I have often found that when depressed it is great to travel as you have minimal responsibilities in transit, leaving behind those at your departure and not having to face anyone else until you arrive at your destination. On the second day of my stay, standing in my dressing-gown in the grounds overlooking the nearby cemetery, I was already formulating a Colditz-like escape.

Life was becoming a board game, a bored game, a trivial pursuit. I simply did not take the opportunity to recover seriously. I even re-enacted the scene from 'One Flew Over the Cuckoo's Nest' when Jack Nicholson manages to avoid swallowing his medication by secreting the pill under his tongue. My deception was discovered by a young nurse who must have seen the film, having monitored the situation from behind the drugs trolley.

I took part in all the group sessions: relaxation, art therapy, morning exercise, more relaxation, games, discussion, some more relaxation – small wonder the staff seemed so laid back.

I avoided my issues by offering support to other patients. I have discovered that Mr Freud called this displacement, replacing an original aim with another, as the first appears too frightening.

I was simply desperate to meet my employment deadline of April 1. Short-term success took precedence over almost inevitable medium-term failure. I was more intent on the ridiculous aim of memorising the contents of 800 pages of the Spring Bookseller than dealing with my emotions.

I was let out with an escort to go into the city centre for a few hours, even revisiting my old place of work to wave a cheery hello. My ex-boss was somewhat taken aback. I no longer avoided the 'loony' on the bus, I was that 'loony'. My clothes were returned after a few days and, when I requested a voluntary discharge on March 28, it was granted.

Even in such a short period I had witnessed some vivid scenes of sadness and madness, which were ingrained onto my memory. These included the real life scenario of patients disturbed by a full moon, a young teenage lad admitted for drinking bleach, an elderly husband watching helplessly and tearfully as his senile wife urinated openly on the dining room floor, plates hurled venomously at mealtimes, a seemingly mild mannered man trying to strangle his wife and staff pursuing a stark naked male patient on a midnight streak around the wards.

I had met my deadline. Even so I was at rock bottom. I had to ask my parents to accompany me and sit outside my new place of work for nearly an hour on my first day. My hands shook in almost uncontrollable spasms, as I clutched at the artificial comfort of my too hot plastic coffee cup.

Staff members introduced themselves. It was a brand new shop, due to open in a couple of weeks. Six months previously I had been controlling all the stock in a busy shop. Now I could barely concentrate enough to dust the shelves. Thankfully the work was quite physically demanding, carrying huge parcels of pristine publications around strangely empty and luxuriously carpeted floors. I can still recall that new carpet smell.

The local builders were completing the final touches. One of them was always cheerful, which I found rather irritating. Amazingly our paths would cross again, as the knotted strings of our lives unravelled.

My colleagues were all very friendly including Amanda, Fiona, Rose, 'Big Steve', 'Little Steve'; a rather common first name I have found, having once played in a five-a-side football team containing four.

The crème-da-la crème of the local book scene, according to management; little did they know of the hidden 'nutter' in their midst. One of my deepest feelings was of isolation, a tortured soul smiling so falsely and cracking jokes.

I was temporarily reconciled with Sue for a fortnight, but after another blazing confrontation, I smashed a plate glass door with my fist, slashing my wrist deliberately. I missed the artery by millimetres. To casualty, to casualty. I was not readmitted to psychiatric care, which perversely, this time, I found quite a relief.

I was put on a cardiogram for a couple of hours, still managing to grab the limelight, when a lead became loose and I was temporarily registered 'dead'. I returned to work the next day, using a facile lie that I'd fallen off a stepladder and into a window. Nobody asked questions.

I was back at my parents' house trying to be as content as possible with the situation. It seemed no more than I deserved. Any communication with my wife by telephone or in person was completely counterproductive and ultimately destructive.

During May I started to write letters. I received no replies. On the evening of Thursday, May 15, I became illogically frantic. I knew my wife was going out for a drink with a mutual male friend. How was I going to stand a chance against this rival. After work I too went for a drink with two female colleagues, possibly out of spite. I wanted to confide in them and spill out all my despair. I couldn't.

While waiting for a bus afterwards in a street that I had walked along thousands of times, I felt that I no longer knew the place. All my bearings had disappeared. I had always liked to travel as long as I could come home. Where was I now? Where the heart is? I felt as though my heart had been ripped out and hung to dry. Maybe it was mixing alcohol with the antidepressants that finally unhinged me, although I only had a pint of lager. I will never know, which is probably just as well. I would not want to be put off the beer.

Just before going to bed I wrote Sue's name and address on a slip of paper, sliding it into my trouser back pocket. No letters, no notes. Tomorrow would be the day.

I awoke the next morning sullen, full of a graphic nightmare involving my wife. Somehow it seemed to justify my fears and therefore even more illogically, my intention. Nevertheless I was beginning to get cold feet. I heard my father starting up the car. He was dropping me off to work as usual.

'Are you going to work today?' questioned my mother as I lay languid across the bed, fully clothed.

'I suppose I had better make the effort', came my hard retort.

Once at work I counted off the hours, then the minutes till noon. I realised with sudden horror that my early lunch break had been changed. The final reprieve that causes the self condemned man to die of heart failure. I became so agitated that I coerced one of my colleagues to swap back.

As noon struck on City Hall clock, I ran out of the shop heading full pelt along the streets that led to St Andrew's multi-storey car park. A different one this time.

Motorists hooted as I swerved between traffic crossing a busy one way street.

'You just wait and see!' I yelled.

I would show them all, whoever they were; my family, my wife, the world? I was overflowing with rage. Nobody really understood. This was it.

I kept running straight through the car park entrance, non-stop up the dozen or so flights, taking the steps two at a time. I was panting for breath as I burst through the wooden swing doors and across the almost deserted roof. A seemingly alien force was willing me to self destruct. I slowed only slightly, but did not dare pause as I mounted the parapet and in one swift motion leapt into oblivion.

Chapter 3
Is it a Bird, Is it a Plane?

'A man was described as seriously ill in hospital last night after plunging from a Norwich multi-storey car park. Mr Stephen* Foyster, aged late twenties, fell from the St Andrew's car park at about 12.30pm yesterday. He was taken to the Norfolk and Norwich Hospital with severe leg injuries. A spokesman for Norwich police said the incident was being investigated'. Eastern Daily Press, May 17, 1986.

I found this piece in the local paper on wind round microfiche at our reference library, when I started the first draft of this book. I had in fact seen the clipping before, when Sue had somewhat ghoulishly brandished it at me in hospital, stating that at last I had now achieved infamy.

I had long lost that particular reminder of my 15 minutes of fame. So it was curious to see it tucked away at the bottom of column six, page 13. It seemed so insignificant compared to the Chernobyl death toll, which in turn had simply passed me by during my particular version of hell.

It was very enlightening to see that the May 20 edition of the EDP had the following front page report: 'Young Suicides on Increase. More and more young people are killing themselves, the Samaritans reported yesterday. The organisation believes the numbers are only the tip of the iceberg, with many more deaths never resulting in suicide verdicts because of the need for clear evidence at inquests.'

Sometimes I still refer to the jump as an 'accident'. I try to gauge the individual's potential reaction, before I explain how I incurred the injuries still obvious when I remove my boots and socks, and even more apparent when walking with the aid of a stick.

It never ceased to amaze me that a young man in his thirties using a walking aid could provide so many conversation openers, running or should I say limping a close second to the English weather.

'What have you been up to then? Skiing accident was it?' If it was just a passing comment, I usually let it drop. If people seemed genuinely concerned and I felt that I could handle their reaction, I told them the truth. Otherwise it was simply an accident. People normally think you mean a road traffic accident. Then I would quickly change the subject to something more 'life and death' like the latest fortunes of Norwich City Football Club.

*Incorrect, Steven is correct.

I can remember landing, but not falling. If my A level physics still holds strong it could only have lasted a couple of seconds. I can still relive hitting the pavement from about 55 feet. Evidently I had launched off from the very highest part and sailed past the back of the art college, which in hindsight must have been extremely distressing for any onlookers, and crashed down just off the main thoroughfare.

All the impact went onto my left foot with my right lower leg buckling under as my torso lurched forward, smashing my chest onto my left knee and thigh. I was still conscious as a few onlookers hastily gathered around in, I guess, various states of shock, amazement and even curiosity.

Somebody kindly put a coat or jacket over me and I distinctly recall someone asking

'Where did he come from?'

'Up there', came an honest reply, presumably pointing skyward. I can afford to be slightly amused by the non-caped crusader scenario now.

An ambulance arrived, bringing with it an amazing coincidence. One of the medics was Claude, my one new friend from the Methodist youth club. He had also been an infrequent customer at the shop where I had worked prior to my current job at Waterstones. He was totally shell-shocked to see me in this state.

'My God Stevie, what have you done?' he cried, in a somewhat unprofessional manner.

Both medics manoeuvred me onto a stretcher and into the ambulance. I began to struggle. Maybe my subconscious was starting to realise that it had not worked; the adrenaline pumped back.

Claude barked at me to keep still. I reluctantly complied. I was losing my grip.

I started to cry. 'I love you Claude' I blubbered.

'Don't be stupid Stevie' he responded. 'I am too ugly'.

Humour, our most precious gift, prevailed. We arrived at the ambulance bay at A & E whereupon I passed out.

On regaining consciousness the first thing my eyes focussed on was a beautiful bouquet in the corner of a small overlit room. I will never forget that sight, so full of vibrant life, contrasting so powerfully with the anaemic decor.

I assumed that the flowers were from my wife or parents. I was astounded to discover that they had been sent by my work colleagues, who had only known me for a few weeks.

It was indeed ridiculous to consider that anyone close to me would be emotionally stable enough to arrange a delivery of flowers. I was told much later that I had been very close to death and even given the last rites by a hospital chaplain. One of my mother's close friends had turned up at the hospital unannounced, to sit in vigil with my parents. People can be incredibly kind.

In fact I had not given any consideration to the impact that the slip of paper with Sue's address would have. Two police officers had arrived on my wife's doorstep. I had wrongly assumed she would be at work with colleagues when I jumped but, ironically, had taken a day's leave.

Although my parents, especially my mother, had been aware that something akin to this was on the cards, they were still walking wrecks.

I was in a side room on my own, off the acute medical ward. I had lost a couple of days.

My hospital notes, copies of which I paid for in 2019, stated:

19-05-86 'Admitted 16-05-86, suicide attempt. Jumped off seventh floor of a car park in Norwich. Several suicide attempts before including slashing of wrist, overdoses.

My injuries were listed as:

1)   Several wedge fractures of lumbar spine
2)   Diastasis of pelvis
3)   Fractured left superior and inferior pubic remus
4)   Dislocation of mid foot on left side
5)   Dilateral calcaneal fractures, grossly communite
6)   Probable rupture bladder or urethra shown on IVU
7)   Possible injuries to chest

It was just as well that I did not know about these for many weeks. My condition was monitored carefully. I had bypassed intensive care via casualty.

Contrary to the engulfing blackness of the previous weeks, I was suddenly deliriously happy to be alive. I asked my dad to bring in lots of 10 pence pieces.

I spent at least half-an-hour telephoning my friends to inform them that I was still in this world. They must have thought I had really lost the plot, as I do not think most of them were aware of the situation.

When Sue left I suddenly felt alone. The consequences of what I had done started to filter through. I was strapped to the bed unable to move from the chest downwards. Presumably this was to prevent my injuries being made any worse, but also possibly to keep me restrained.

I asked to use the telephone trolley again. I rang Sue and begged her to return. This she did, I know not how, given the exhausted state she was in. I wanted her to stay the night but obviously she could not. I was no longer on the critical list. I started to waiver between delirium and hysteria. She called the staff nurse and I was sedated.

I developed severe breathing difficulties during the evening. My notes from the end of May 19 said that a pneumothorax was expected on clinical grounds. I was rushed to the Elizabeth Fry Critical Care unit. One of my lungs had indeed collapsed. Due to internal bleeding I received two transfusions.

I have never been able to reconcile the Jehovah Witness stance on this. All life is precious. I had the dubious honour of being the first patient through a brand new catscan prior to it being officially opened by a member of the royal family, typical of yours truly.

While being shunted extremely slowly through the tube, I was rather bewildered to hear music. Perhaps I was about to join a celestial chorus? I was later assured that background musak had been playing to relieve the stress. Somehow that objective had not quite been achieved.

Back at the Elizabeth Fry unit I was put on a respirator. I was fed intravenously with a milky liquid. I could feel its coolness entering my veins, a bizarre sensation. Communication was via the written word or gesticulation. I was allowed to suck a sliver of ice cube every half hour which alleviated my searing throat. As a special treat the nursing staff occasionally produced an orange flavoured cube or a damp lemony swab, the poor man's sherbet dip.

I had to be turned hourly to prevent bed sores. I came to dread this procedure. Severe bruising covered all my legs and most of my lower and middle back. Every so often I was lifted onto a sturdy sheet by two nurses and swivelled over onto my front, with the procedure reversed an hour later.

My screams could evidently be heard outside the unit's double doors. I simply cannot envisage how survivors of such tragedies as the King's Cross or Bradford City FC fires coped with the incessant trauma. The ability for human beings to work through and even work with extreme physical pain never ceases to amaze me.

Get well cards started to arrive. I was too numb to take in most of the messages. I do recall one very flowery poem from a woman in the church where Bob and Ann worshipped. It rambled on about the eternal forgiveness from that nice man Jesus. Frankly it nearly made me throw up.

'Too late pal' was my cynical riposte. However I was stunned to receive such warm wishes from churchgoers who I had only met fleetingly. Did they send them out of a sense of obligation I mused, even more cynically? Yet, virtual strangers were praying for insignificant me. My hard as nails mother-in-law lit a candle for me in St John's Roman Catholic Cathedral.

I remember very little from the five days spent in Elizabeth Fry, as I drifted in and out of consciousness, the pain mercifully numbed by very strong analgesics. Memories include a nurse revising the highway code prior to her driving test, someone vacuuming the floor to a pristine sheen, weeping relatives paying their last respects as there was nowhere else to lay their father's body and the heart rending screams of a very young child admitted with bad burns.

Somehow that toddler's suffering brought my situation into perspective. During the afternoon, before he was admitted, a very kind nurse had offered to read to me in the evening, as I was sleeping very badly at night, despite the sedatives. I was relishing the thought of this, having been an avid reader from a young age. Then this emergency took over.

At first I felt cheated, then overwhelmed by the cries of anguish from this innocent child, separated from me by a mere partition. I even tried to lend my bunny mascot, but the child was understandably inconsolable until the pain relief hit home and the crying subsided into sobs and finally silence. A toddler on a cross. An almost unbearable thought which did not seem very flowery at all.

On the fifth day I was due to move back to the side ward. Mid-morning a doctor removed the respirator and tested my breathing capacity. The cool air scorched down into my lungs, as I struggled with the respiratory monitor.

'That's not good enough' he voiced, testily. Try some breathing techniques for the next few hours'.

So I did. Over and over and over and over and over and over again, using the respirator for support in between deep breathing sessions. I was so desperate to get back to the womb-like solitude of the side room. When the doctor returned I almost blew the machine across the room.

'I think that is OK,' he smiled wryly.

The next morning I was bed-wheeled back to my beloved room. Before I left the unit I joked with the nurses that one day, when I could dance again, we would have a big party. They laughed too, but in a 'we had better humour this one manner'.

Chapter 4

Guilt is a Four Letter Word

My triumphant return to semi-isolation was short-lived. Later the same day it was decided to move me to a main ward, sharing with five other men. Although my physical condition had stabilised somewhat, I was scared that I might not be accepted by other patients, once they inevitably discovered how I had incurred my injuries. This was of course very judgmental of me.

As it happened, the room was mainly inhabited by much older men, who were generally too ill to communicate, so my fears lay lurking, temporarily unfounded. On the second night two porters wheeled in a young lad of about 20, who had just received an emergency below knee amputation, following a hit and run on a dark, but straight country road.

The next day police officers visited to question the poor lad. He had been holidaying on the Norfolk Broads and had some drinks before crossing the road with his mates. He did not even spot the car.

That afternoon, worse was to follow, when the surgeon realised that the operation hadn't been completely successful and a further amputation, slightly higher, was necessary.

Not a murmur. Was this stoic bravery of the highest level? However, when his parents arrived from Yorkshire, he almost immediately started to spew out a torrential gush of pent up anger, mainly aimed at his stricken mother. You often hurt the ones...

In the evening when he returned from further surgery I offered M a few comforting words and decided to share my dark secret. His reaction was sympathetic and my guilt factor fell from 10 to 9.5.

I was not receiving any psychiatric help or counselling at this crucial time. My parents virtually begged for someone from the clinic to visit. The powers that be eventually relented. Evidently I talked coherently to said person for an hour, yet I remember absolutely nothing from the meeting. There was no follow up.

A few days later M and me were moved to a different ward, so that we could be with patients nearer our own age. Again the sulphurous guilt started to froth up from the pit of my stomach. After all, injuries often pre-empted the weather as conversation openers, especially as when lying flat you could not see much out of the windows.

There were two victims of motorcycle accidents, Kev a young lorry driver and family man, who had been trapped in his cab for three hours before being cut out and, worst of all, an eight year-old whose leg had been snapped in another hit and run. He was to remain in the same bed for three months.

I felt terrible and kept my peace. Look at what had happened to these innocents compared to what I had inflicted on myself. What would good old God feel about that? I had mutilated a very healthy image. In line with my waivering agnosticism, I did not believe I would receive divine forgiveness for what I had done, even if it existed.

Kev's wife and young children made the trek from their home in Humberside twice a week. Robert, his young son, who was about five, wandered unselfconsciously between patients, casually chatting. He called my bandaged leg 'my poorly foot'. I just wanted to hide away and cry, but hospital bed linen is very thin.

Then during a consultant's ward round one Monday, I started to hear that some of the young bikers were making their second or even third appearance on the orthopaedic circuit. One had been strongly advised not to get back onto any motorcycle for some time, if ever, but had recklessly ignored the warnings. I started to ponder how many accidents were actually caused by an amount of choice. Guilt factor now 8.5.

I was introduced to a lovely smiley man named Lesley Ward, one of the hospital chaplains. He called by one day just to ask how I was coping. I admitted to feeling fairly awful, but did not want to talk about the issues. Lesley did not press the point. He enquired if I would like to receive communion, as I was down on my medical notes as Church of England by default. I guess from time to time the C of E is perceived as a waivering institution, so maybe I would feel quite at home.

I was not a communicant member. I had received infant baptism at our local parish church but surely I had not jumped through any of the other pre-required ecclesiastical hoops .This did not seem to matter to Lesley; 15 love to the divine one. However, I had always considered that it was a rather superstitious ritual when viewed from my pew at St Johns - 15 -all. Yet I had nothing to lose - 30-15 . It could not do any harm - 40-15. Maybe it was a conversion trick - 40-30. Nevertheless I agreed. Game to Omniscient.

So, every Tuesday morning at 6.45am, I received a wafer but no wine. Lesley's non-judgmental attitude and the symbolism of a broken body entering mine dropped the guilt level to below five, yet I still felt a chill factor swirling around my soul from time to time.

I could not explain and I still cannot adequately express why receiving communion has been so special to me. Maybe it is because I first experienced it at a very vulnerable time and Christ first offered it at a very, very vulnerable time for him.

I do not think you are supposed to explain or theologically dissect what happens, simply experience it. I can look back to very special times as everybody can - that passionate kiss, that overhead goal, that wonderful holiday, that amazing sunset and sometimes such life-enhancing experiences can be replicated in a similar fashion along the winding road.

The wonder for me is that every communion service that I have attended with different denominations, has moved me in some way, often incredibly so, despite any horrendous hymns and tedious sermons. I have gone months without receiving the sacraments and have received them thrice in 48 hours. For me it is not the frequency that matters, but simply the immense privilege to be with Christ and to re-enact that first supper, when he tried to prepare for his trials and torment, possibly hoping that his earthly mission had not been entirely fruitless.

I do not believe in transubstantiation, but do not decry those who do, as long they do not try to enforce that particular doctrine on me. Sharing the eucharist is for me simultaneously awe inspiring and humbling, totally encapsulating the divine-human relationship of Jesus.

Nevertheless, despite the church's desperate attempts to get all the words right in the correct order, the sacrament remains a mystery. Amen to that.

Physically I was more stable, my system pumped with antibiotics, painkillers, sleeping pills - a pharmaceutical cocktail that was shaken to make me not stir.

My pelvis had been pulled apart by about four inches. So, I was put into traction with a metal cradle over me, weighted on either side, in the hope that the bones would pull and knit back together.

I had been advised that I would need to lie still for six weeks while the load was gradually increased. My shins were still so swollen with bruising that my father commented that it looked like I had wellington boots on. I now wish he had taken a photograph of them for posterity.

Boredom began to set in. Dad brought in a portable television, but as the pressure on my pelvis increased, my concentration threshold diminished accordingly. I watched very little, the exploits of the England football team at the World Cup did nothing to raise my spirits. It became very important to stick to a ritual routine to survive each static 16-hour day.

Curtain up at 6am, cup of tea, blood pressure and temperature, breakfast, drugs trolley, wash (not very much for me), sweets and paper trolley, coffee, drugs trolley, lunch, visitors from 2pm to 4pm, cup of tea, blood pressure and temperature, supper, visitors from 6pm to 8pm, hot drink, bed rub to prevent sores, then hopefully sweet dreams. Any delays caused me disproportionate irritation, as I was totally reliant on other people.

It was excessively hot on the ward. Flaming June was actually living up to its potential. All the patients needed electric fans close at hand to survive the daylight hours.

I was living between painkillers. The drug dosage became so high that I regularly experienced hallucinogenic dreams, often in the style of Lewis Carroll's Wonderland. It is a shame that the visuals of dreams cannot yet be transferred direct from the brain onto a computer screen - maybe only a matter of time?

One afternoon I flicked on the TV to discover the joys of Chariots of Fire. It seemed to be hinting that all is possible against the odds and that just maybe divine inspiration can help you along the way a wee bit. The reading from Harold Abraham's memorial service has stayed with me:

'The Lord is the everlasting God, the creator of the ends of the Earth. He will not grow tired or weary and His understanding no one can fathom. He gives strength to the weary and increases the power of the weak. Even youths grow tired and weary and young men stumble and fall, But those who hope in the Lord will renew their strength. They will soar on wings like eagles, they will run and not grow weary, they will walk and not be faint' – Book of Isaiah, Chapter 40, verse 28 onwards.

The cards continued to pour in from family, friends, colleagues and cousins that I had not seen for years. The nurses stuck them onto the inside of an outfacing window next to my corner bed, so that my parents could locate me as they approached the hospital entrance up a long concrete ramp.

Mum and dad visited once or twice a day, hardly ever missing. There was often virtually nothing new to report, so conversation would quickly dry up. I never knew and still do not really know how much my actions caused them to suffer, both in the short and long-term.

Those very dark days were never really spoken of. Maybe the need to close as much of it off as possible is how they coped with it.

There were plenty of other visitors, sometimes too many. Yet I never eclipsed an 18 year-old fellow patient, who had more than a dozen groupies buzzing noisily around his bed. Sister hastily intervened to disperse the swarm.

I received so much encouragement. Tim Waterstone, head of the bookshop chain for which I had worked for less than two months, sent me a hand-written letter of good wishes, promising to keep my job open for as long as it took me to recover. I was still on full pay and dumbstruck, which believe me was very out of character. Years later I read in a Sunday supplement that he followed the Christian faith.

My very good friend Keith, who I had known since the age of five, called to see me every day without fail, sometimes even squeezing in a visit before an evening cricket match. I did not know at the time that his grandfather was also hospitalised following a major heart attack, from which he was not going to recover.

My ex-boss visited, very bravely I thought, as we had not exactly parted on the best of terms.

' You know Steve' he admitted, ' there were quite a few of us who pushed you towards the edge'. This was another very potent dose of anti-guilt serum.

Nevertheless, I was still feeling terrible about how I had treated my wife. I expressed these concerns to a student nurse, who very kindly took extra time to massage my bruised feet in the hope of improving the circulation. She shared with me how appallingly her boyfriend had treated her throughout their relationship and he had not been suffering from depression. I slowly began to grasp that maybe in my new vocabulary, guilt should be a four letter word.

Chapter 5

My God, My God, Why Hast Thou Forsaken Me?

The weights on either side of the pelvic cross were still being increased, to hopefully finally bring the pelvis together, like those last few turns when you burr the screw. Despite copious analgesics, the pain across the sacroiliac bones was at times almost intolerable.

Then I made a fortuitous discovery. I found that I was able to slide off the cylindrical solid metal 'cheese' weights from the top of their rods. So, I put up with severe discomfort that the little beauties induced during the day. Then during the night, when I could not sleep, I surreptitiously removed a couple of 'cheeses', secreting them by my bed and replaced them before the 6am reveille.

However nursing notes of June 12 and 14 show that nothing went unnoticed from the night shift angels: ' Patient continues to remove weights'.

They decided to hang the weights slightly out of reach from my virtually prone body. The next evening I literally begged Keith to take some off the weights off. Now Keith could be an adventurous bloke, to put it mildly, but even he drew the line on this occasion. It was all in my best interests.

So late that night I used all my available energy to swing up again and again to eventually remove two of the demons. The next morning I awoke in a state of smug satisfaction only to discover to my horror that the weights had not only been replaced, but stuck together with yards and yards of sticky tape. The feisty Florence Nightingales had won.

Bowel movement, or lack of it, in a room of immobile men can rate highly as a topic of conversation. Grown males can become totally panic-stricken at the thought of using, or not being able to use a bedpan. Each day of constipation was monitored as we did not go through the motions. The graphic descriptions of the final results even made some of the nurses blush. Unfortunately, as I was lying completely still, apart from washes and bed rubs to prevent sores, my digestive system did not stand a chance.

However much I tried using the bedpans, which proved very rough and sore against my bruised buttocks, I could yield no results. The days ticked by. No need to worry the nurses assured me, but I started to become paranoid. I tried both suppositories and enemas. I became quite frantic with anxiety caused by the pain constantly building in my abdomen.

Finally after five days, an angel of mercy called Jane fetched the senior nurse, Brian, who decided the waste should be removed manually. Now one might be on the best of speaking terms with someone, but having their fingers pushed up your rectum is slightly more personal. Holding my father's hand, waiting for Brian to stretch into his sterilised gloves, I certainly felt that I had hit a new level of vulnerability. I was semi-naked with a steel cross of 'torture' pulling me apart emotionally and was stripped of all my dignity. But surely someone had been here before?

So often crucifixes depict a nicely balanced body in silver on a worthy piece of wood, with limbs symmetrically laid out and neatly holed appendages. Thank goodness for the gnarled effigies of total anguish and despair that seek to depict the true horror behind one of the most agonising forms of execution.

Six hours of unrelenting heat, sweat, drying blood, suffocating thirst and the merciless attention of flies. Six hours was quick compared to many. Perhaps Christ had the extreme urge to relieve himself. Maybe under the unbelievable physical, mental and spiritual pain he did. That sort of 'obscenity' tends to be glossed over in a squeaky clean rendering of a Gospel that is often earthy.

Such physically intimate passages are one of the reasons that I still find an often visceral gospel narrative so compulsive to follow. What other religion depicts the son of God wiping spittle on someone's eyes to cure them of blindness?

It was small wonder that Jesus cried out to his father for forsaking him. Although I did not utter those words, I felt abandoned. There was indeed a severe blockage, which was very carefully and expertly removed. Despite the anxiety and embarrassment, I remain eternally grateful to Brian and his nursing assistant James for the compassion and tenderness they exhibited.

Maybe David Broome's hands were still encircling me. Of course to show such compassion you do not have to label yourself a Christian or follower of any faith or none. However later I was interested to discover that Brian was a regular churchgoer.

Indeed these Christians were appearing at very opportune moments: Bob and Ann, David Broome, Claude, Lesley Ward and now Brian. Somehow they were entirely breaking my mental mould of the 'we go to church but let us not get our hands dirty' brigade. In Brian's case this was literally true, notwithstanding the latex gloves.

I was finally able to master the bedpan, which I eventually had to befriend rather than fear. There were of course lighthearted moments. A teenager called Carl had plaster the full length of his leg, following what sounded to me a rather risk-laden motorcycle accident. My guilt must have been evaporating like the early morning mist. He developed a highly irritating itch halfway down his thigh, which he could not quite get to, even with the aid of a somewhat dangerous knitting needle.

Eventually the nurses took pity on him and called in the hospital plasterer. He duly arrived brandishing a substantial circular saw on the end of an electric drill. Carl's face was a picture as he no doubt envisaged a rerun of the Texas Chainsaw Massacre.

Seeing his terror the plasterer and subsequently the rest of us delighted in winding up Carl even further. Nevertheless it was with excessive relief that he was able to rescratch his flesh once a neat two-inch square had been safely and expertly cut.

Matt of the myriad visitors, had a nasty wound, which was bandaged and held to his rather hairy legs with a copious dose of sticking plaster. The day arrived when the wound had to be redressed. So the plaster had to come off. He was understandably concerned about this, getting into quite a lather. When the nurse arrived she easily placated him with soothing tones.

'Oh it is all right', she assured. 'We have a special method for removing this stuff here called the Zoff method.'

' What's that?' enquired Matt timidly.

With one brisk efficient flourish she stripped off the whole lot, together with no doubt, several hundred of Matthew's hair follicles.

'There you are, it's Zoff', she chortled.

He was speechless, shocked with the pain. Needless to say the conversation between patient and carer was less than cordial for several days.

During my time in traction I did in fact receive some minor surgery on my left foot. A four-inch thin metal pin was inserted to straighten some of the bones. My left ankle had received multiple fractures. Any major attempt at surgery would probably have caused the whole foot to disintegrate.

The morning dawned when the pin had to be removed. Mike a young doctor was to carry out this task. I must admit he appeared unduly nervous about what he explained would be a very quick, painless and simple procedure. I was to be given a local anaesthetic in the foot to avoid any discomfort and Mike would slide out the pin with his fingers, or if necessary, a pair of pliers.

I was wheeled into a store room behind the nurses' station. After the injection had taken hold, Mike started to pull at the pin, whilst I lay prostrate on the bed. After a few minutes he had to resort to the pliers but several more minutes pulling proved equally fruitless. Mike suggested that we needed something or someone to hold the foot steady to give better leverage.

Louise, one of the student nurses was summoned. She held the foot. Mike tugged, to no avail. The anaesthetic was now starting to wear off and the skin around the pin was beginning to bruise due to the constant pulling.

Mike decided on one last effort. It must have been a bizarre sight, me holding onto a nearby couch, Louise actually lying face down across my legs and Mike huffing, puffing and exuding quite a lot of sweat. All in vain. I was wheeled back onto the ward.

Mike decided to seek advice from his registrar and return the next day. I could hardly wait.

The next morning Mike duly appeared brimming with confidence. I was given another injection and, within a couple of minutes, the devilish pin slid out. Evidently he had been advised that the trick was to wiggle rather than wrench.

July 14 - traction was to cease. Early in the morning the cradle was removed. It was absolute bliss to slide up and down and to turn more easily. I was naturally looking forward to progressing further, after so many weeks of immobility.

My consultant, an extremely competent, yet rather dry orthopaedic surgeon, included me in his ward round. The pelvic repair had evidently gone quite well. I would soon be able to get into a wheelchair. I felt exhilarated. All the perseverance had been worth it.

I enquired when I would be able to try walking again.

He looked at me quite clinically, with a mixture of disbelief and astonishment, before uttering, 'I am afraid you have to come to terms with the fact that you will probably remain in a wheelchair for the rest of your life'.

I was stunned. It was as if this man had hurled a bucket of cold vomit over the remainder of my life, without even giving me a chance. I am sure my hurt was evident to the rest of the team around my bed, which included a young doctor and a physiotherapist.

I was too overwhelmed to react very much. I just stuttered, 'Oh, I see'.

Then he was off to the next patient, the next case. During the ensuing half-hour the real effect of the 'top man's' prognosis began to sink in. I could not contain my emotion.

Racked with tears, I pushed my alarm bell and between sobs managed to communicate to the staff nurse that I needed the phone. She was most concerned at my distress and very kindly held my hand for a while.

I called my parents. They came immediately. I rang my wife. She promised to visit later. By the time mum and dad arrived my angst had turned to anger. I was being cheated after being a 'model patient'.

This fait accompli had been thrust upon me unannounced before I had even sat in the wheelchair. My parents demanded to see the consultant but he refused. The young doctor acquiesced. After a lengthy chat in a side room all three emerged.The doctor was very considerate and even apologised for the manner in which the matter had been handled.

' However', he explained, 'you have four major injuries: a broken pelvis, compacted lumbar vertebrae, multiple fractures of the left ankle and probable severance of the sciatic nerve causing paralysis of the lower right leg. Any one of these could prevent you from getting out of a wheelchair.'

He added that in the medium term future, if I had a prosthesis fitted to my right leg, I might eventually be able to walk a bit with the aid of a stick, probably with quite a limp. It was just as well that I did not realise at the time that he was hinting at a false lower limb rather than callipers.

Dad tried to make light of it. 'You could have a smart cane with a brass top.'

'Yes, but what about the football and tennis?' I wailed totally unrealistically, my hysteria bypassing the intermediary stages of standing, walking and running.

'You have to realise, Steve that you are very lucky to be alive.' was his caring and realistic response.

I knew I was asking far too much. I had enjoyed hundreds of games of tennis over the previous 12 years and too many football matches to remember from the age of nine, without incurring any serious injuries.

When my wife visited I reverted to the woe is me scenario. ' If it is so useless why don't they just cut it off?' I hissed.

She shot a furtive glance at M. 'Do not even think about it' she glared.

I was suitably abashed. With rather sobering thoughts I drifted into sleep later that evening. God seemed to be with me, but I was asking too much.... wasn't I?

Chapter 6
Never Let It Be Said

Billy, my paternal grandfather had a saying which he used when presented with a challenge, such as when he and Ethel were faced with a particular nasty incline whilst cycling in their younger days. 'Never let it be said that it cannot be done, or at least we had a good try'. As I was growing up this family motto was often repeated by their daughter Audrey and it has stuck with me.

I awoke the next morning slightly more accepting of the situation. At least the demon cheeses had departed . Soon I would be able to get into the promised land of the wheelchair. I had even beeen able to partake of a proper bath for the first time in eight weeks, much to the relief of the nurses, no doubt.

I had received some blissful hair washes over the back of my bed which were real luxuries to look forward to, but a full length bath was something special. So it was not all doom and gloom. As they say at the end of the best irreligious films, sometimes you have to look on the bright side of life.

During the day some very significant developments unfurled. Firstly the senior physiotherapist, Sue Christie called by to see me. She explained the issues involved and potential problems that might occur when I transferred to a wheelchair. As I was still very vulnerable and unable to stand I would have to be carried out of and back into bed by two nurses, using an Australian lift. I had not heard of this procedure, but as long as they were careful 'down under', I really was not bothered what they used.

I started to tentatively broach the consultant's prognosis. Sue suggested that it was just possible that the sciatic nerve had been very badly bruised, rather than totally ruptured.

'So what difference will that make?' I almost demanded in my desperation for further blue sky news.

'Well', she continued calmly, trying not to raise my hopes too high, 'the nerve could regenerate, given time'.

'What timescale are we talking about?'

'If the nerve has say five millimetres worth of damage, it could grow back one millimetre per year.'

'But that is five years.' I cried, my junior school times table still in fine fettle.

'I cannot wait that long, I have a job to go to,' I protested.

'I am afraid nature takes its time,' mused Sue.

So that was that. Yet it was a glimmer of hope. Sometimes you have to breathe on a spark to get it glowing.

My wife visited in the afternoon. She was positive that I would walk again. I thought rather callously that this assurance might be borne more of guilt than actual conviction. However I did recall that in the past she had exhibited a sixth sense, once coming to meet me at a totally different location in London to the one that we had arranged, simply because she felt I would be there - Baker Street tube station. So, the game might again be afoot.

Then she produced the coup de grâce.

'Here you are', she said somewhat triumphantly. 'Someone else believes that you will do it.'

It was a letter from a third Sue, the woman who had written the horrendously flowery Jesus poem and who worshipped at the same church as Bob and Ann. In her latest epistle she explained how she had received a vision of me trolling down her church in a wheelchair, suddenly stop, get up and walk. Well I have to admit that against my better cynicism, I was uncharacteristically impressed, almost exhilarated.

Yet surely I had to dismiss this as totally crazy. A top orthopaedic surgeon had only the day before virtually written me off in the erect posture stakes. How could I possibly choose to believe the religious ramblings of this woman? If I did take her vision on board, how would I and she react to my situation if I failed in my quest for the Holy Grail?

I gave the letter back to my wife for unsafe keeping. I have never seen it again. Nevertheless, just before the diazepam took effect that night, I was still pondering on the bizarre content of the seemingly mad missive.

The next day was wheelchair celebration day. An Australian lift consisted of two often slight nurses, forming a cradle with their arms on which I sat. In this fashion I was hoisted off the bed and into the chair, and vice versa on return. Although the lift felt very safe I did fear for the future of the nurses' backs at times. Small wonder that spinal injury is the most common complaint in their profession.

It was truly wonderful to be mobile, ferreting down the corridor to the nurses' station and back. Nevertheless it was very painful. The bruising, although greatly improved, made itself known in no uncertain terms.

My body had not been accustomed to the upright sitting position for several weeks. I was advised to stay out of bed for about an hour. Given my tenacity, or stubbornness, depending on your viewpoint, I managed nearly two. The time out included the blessed bath, which was exceedingly refreshing once I had managed the rigmarole of being winched in on a very hard plastic seat that did no favours to my wasted backside. I also had a plastic bin bag taped over my left foot to protect the wound. It was however still bordering on nirvana.

The catheter was removed, giving me the first chance for two months to pee under my own volition. Given my pelvic injuries, it was likely that I would find this very difficult, maybe even impossible. I approached the toilet cubicle with both expectation and trepidation. I passed water first time. Sister was amazed. The consultant almost smiled. Perhaps I should have bottled it for posterity; the smile that is.

In the afternoon my grandmother and her older sister Hilda dropped by to find me sitting in the wheelchair eating my tea. I had decided to return to it for a brief time, so that Keith, who had been so loyal and consistent in his visitations, could see what I had achieved during the day.

Ethel had visited once before, as I was just going into traction. She had been so grateful that my face had not been injured. In fact it was quite astonishing that only two of my front teeth had been slightly chipped.

As the sisters were about to take their leave I told my grandmother, quite spontaneously, that I would walk out of the hospital. I could not really gauge her reaction. She had never doubted me before, but now she seemed unsure. About a year later she confided in me that she had thought it was a completely crazy statement.

Waiting for Keith, the pain increased. Why is exquisite such an apt adjective to describe a high level of pain, unless you are a masochist? I felt physically sick and I was sweating copiously when Keith arrived. He was totally astounded. It was wonderful to share such a joyful moment together.

'Now that you are mobile, we can get out and celebrate,' he enthused.

'What do you mean? 'I queried, probably already half there in my mind, given that one topic was always high on his agenda.

'There are plenty of decent pubs round these parts' Keith explained. ' I am sure we can wangle a swift half during evening visiting.'

My assumption had been proved correct. Yet, I was more than hesitant. Certainly there would be no imbibing tonight, I was exhausted. However the prospect of a pint of the amber nectar was very tempting. Never let it be said.

Chapter Seven
Get Off Thy Bed

Well, we did, in fact 'escape' on a couple of occasions to local hostelries - the Rose Tavern and the Kimberley Arms. Having checked that a modicum of alcohol would not be detrimental to my medication, which had reduced substantially, Keith used to tip a wink to sister, telling her that we were off for a spin round the park. She would wink back in conspiratorial silence.

Sister Wake certainly lived up to her name and was aware of everything that happened or was about to happen on Brooke Ward. She was attentive, yet never flustered, despite the non-stop demands of immobilised men, a team of student nurses and the small matter that her daughter was about to get married.

It was not always easy to go through the narrow entrances of the nearby pubs. On one occasion we had to sit outside, unprotected from the elements. It looked a bit menacing above and we did not have a coat or umbrella between us.

As the rain lashed down, bouncing into our half-drained beer glasses balanced on a wooden table, we started to laugh somewhat hysterically.

'What mad buggers we are,' I shouted.

'Yes, but at least we are living,' Keith announced.

Indeed. The rain felt wonderful. After weeks and weeks of the stifling artificial air of the ward, I had almost forgotten the sensation. And it could only improve the quality of the Norwich bitter.

When we returned, somewhat bedraggled, the nurse on duty quipped, 'Enjoy your walk in the park then?'

The ward, however, seemed somewhat subdued. We had missed all the drama. The crash team had been called in to stem a suspected heart attack and Billy, an elderly patient, had passed away silently. It was as if he had just given up the will to live - too much like hard work.

Late that night after lights out, M broke the silence. ' You know, about Billy. It makes you think, doesn't it?'

It certainly did.

I still vividly remember the first time that I ventured out in my wheelchair a week previously. My father pushed me purposefully out through the main exit to confront blazing sunlight hammering off the concrete. Everything was so loud, so haphazard and so real after the cottonwool cocoon of hospital routine.

Although I was getting quite expert at manoeuvring the wheelchair, I still declined to perform wheelies and other acrobatics, as perpetrated by the young immobilised motorcyclists. I felt that I had taken enough risks, at least for the time being.

Yet, it was in the chair that I soon experienced one of those life flashing in front of your eyes moments. M's parents and his rather doddery grandfather were visiting. The old man was intent on taking the 'boys' out into the hospital grounds for a breath of fresh air. The public lifts were out of order, so we had to hijack the one used by porters. Maybe we should have taken this as a sign.

To start with all went well, as our little entourage ventured outside, down a concrete ramp, through the car park towards a secluded garden complete with a lily pond. It was when M's grandad spotted the frog that the trouble began. He insisted that I get a better look, endeavouring to drag my wheelchair over a large kerbstone, onto the grass.

As the tipping wheelchair started to overbalance, I stared skyward, panic stricken, waiting for the crunch of my descending head and neck as it hit the concrete. Surely I would avoid another mess?

Mercifully, M's father grabbed the back of the chair in the nick of time. I made sure he pushed me back to the ward. So now I had become scared of a four rather than a 50 foot drop. I guess I was glad to be alive.

One sunny afternoon my brother Roger, younger by four years and another loving family member that I had not considered prior to my suicide attempt, arrived at the same time as Sue my wife. We went on a wheelchair expedition to the nearby Jenny Lind Park. It was more grassy than now, with the childrens' play area. I had mixed emotions. When had we three last been together? No doubt on a happier occasion, yet we were all still alive and the world still turned - swings and roundabouts.

It had been pointed out by Mike the 'wiggle the pin doctor' that when I did finally attempt to stand independently, the pain in my mangled feet might prove intolerable. I was suffering from a dropped right foot due to the lack of active nerve.

The 'foot massage nurse' found me a stout board to place at the bottom of my bed to support the drop. It gave me an idea. Lying fully prone on my back, I pressed as hard as I could manage against the wood with both feet. It did not feel too painful. I knew that being horizontal exerted much less pressure than being in the vertical, but I treasured my secret, like a little boy reading illicitly by torchlight under the bedclothes.

My consultant arrived rather briskly one morning and announced that in three weeks I would be transferred to Mundesley Rehabilitation Hospital on the north Norfolk coast. It was hoped that the physiotherapists and occupational therapists would improve my mobility to help me live independently.

I was determined to meet this deadline and it was a great boost when Sue Christie suggested that some remedial work in the hydrotherapy pool would do me no harm.

I had also been moved to a different bed on the other side of the room, giving me a better view of the outside world. I practised sitting upright to strengthen my back, using the amount of a tall chimney that I could see to gauge my progress. Things were obviously looking up.

I was regularly wheeled down to the pool situated in the hospital basement by a porter and then winched into the water by a lovely lady called Maggie who coincidentally had the same birth date. She nicknamed me 'Scorpio'.

Maggie had worked in the hydrotherapy team for many years, helping patients in and out of the pool, assisting them with undressing and dressing. She still revelled in the vital role she played in many patients' recovery process.

I was quite reticent about being lowered into water as I am a virtual non-swimmer. In fact in a moment of panic I could probably give a lump of concrete a race to the bottom. However I felt quite secure once in the pool, as I was aided across the widths and lengths by the buoyancy of the two physios.

It was truly uplifting to stand clinging onto the side of the pool, with water easing the pressure on my legs and feet. So, maybe replicating the process on terra firma was a possibility.

Meanwhile on the domestic front I decided to try some handwashing, even though it was only a pair of socks. It still gave me a great deal of satisfaction to wheel myself to a communal sink and then to the ward's spin dryer.

Sister remarked, with her tongue halfway up her cheek, that it was indeed good to see me pulling my weight at last. As I wheeled back past the female ward I was also congratulated on my progress by a kindly-looking elderly, but sprightly patient. I fell into conversation with Mildred and we soon discovered that we had a mutual enjoyment of scrabble.

We spent many happy hours in pursuit of the elusive seven letter word. I think Mildred usually enjoyed the encounters more than me; she nearly always won and I considered myself no walkover.

'I think I have a little something here,' she would coo innocently, finding a triple word score for the third successive time.

I was often exasperated, but never cross. Life was now too precious to worry about losing a board game. Life was no longer a bored game. There were much bigger stakes at hand.

Sue Christie was very pleased with my progress. I felt that she was pushing the powers that be to encourage me onwards and upwards. I had not dared to broach the dream of walking out of the Norfolk and Norwich, but with about two weeks to my discharge date, I decided to take the lead. I expected her to object. Instead she simply agreed that it was a distinct feasibility, given my recent recovery rate.

She explained that I would need to build up my arms to be able to walk on parallel bars and then use elbow crutches. I was provided with very strong metal springs which were tethered to my metal head board so that I could workout whenever I wanted. I spent many hours trying to imitate Arnold Schwarzenegger. I would be back.

'Aah, the old parallel bars Kato,' as Inspector Clouseau might have quipped.

Sue told me to wheel the chair to one end of the bars. We were set up in the TV room - an athletics meeting was being broadcast. Very tentatively, under expert guidance, I eased myself into an upright position. It was a truly thrilling sensation, the closest I have ever come to feeling physically born again.

I gradually let my feet touch the floor, without exerting much pressure. Not much discomfort. I felt totally elated that my assumptions had been at least partially confirmed. However, It was still incredibly hard to drag myself along the bars, despite all the arm preparation work.

'This is taking me as much effort as him,' I gestured at Seb Coe, just completing a rapid 800 metres.

'Everything is relative,' Sue pointed out. I do not think any wiser words concerning recovery have ever been spoken.

Before being allowed onto crutches I had to be fitted with a plastic brace on my dropped right foot, which would hopefully prevent my leg from buckling under me when I tried to walk.

Sue wheeled me down to the hospital workshop, in the bowels of the oldest part of the hospital along walls of Victorian green tiles and under badly lagged pipes, that surely would not pass health and safety muster these days. It was assumed we would have to get one especially made.

'How long will that take?' I almost demanded. Tempus fugit.

'Oh about a week', was Sue's casual response, rather sensing my apprehension.

A week would be too long, I reflected in stubborn silence. I needed ten days crutch practise prior to discharge. How stupid of me to have such ridiculous unrealistic plans.

The engineer was very amenable, yet also very much doubted if he had the required fit in stock. He scurried off for a rummage around. I did not know what to think. Sometimes it is indeed easier to bear a realistic despair than an improbable hope.

He returned with a left foot plastic cast that he could bend and amend immediately. I do not know who was most amazed out of the three of us. As I am typing this I am still feeling very retrospective goosebumps. Another coincidence?

I also needed a pair of shoes to wear to prevent sliding while manoeuvring myself on crutches. Given the amount of swelling caused by rapid calcification around the left ankle, I was dubious that I had anything that would fit. I only possessed one pair of shoes and one pair of trainers. The shoes were not a very pleasant reminder as I had worn them for the leap. Dad brought in the trainers. They fitted. It was getting a bit Cinderellaesque.

And for the next trick, elbow crutches, which looked particularly daunting when I watched fellow patients on their trial 'runs' or more often than not, 'staggers'. I did a few hundred arm pulls for good measure. Then the day dawned.

I telephoned my wife to see if she would like to witness a piece of Steve Foyster history. She was rather laissez-faire, finding it extremely difficult to comprehend why I was trying so hard now, when I had so little, as I had tried to destroy everything when I supposedly had so much. I had no appropriate answer. Maybe it was because I had 'cheated' death that I now believed I had nothing to lose and hopefully lots to gain.

Anyway she happened to have a day off and agreed to visit. I was quite disappointed with her reaction, but tried not to let that detract from the moment.

I realised some time later that it was her way of gradually withdrawing from our relationship. I now admire her greatly from her honest stance, when she could have been falsely empathetic. Honesty is always the best policy as I later learnt as an insurance salesman.

As I was heading for the TV room my aunt Audrey and her husband Brian arrived unexpectedly. I hoisted myself slightly precariously onto the crutches. Under Sue Christie's instructions I took one step forward, before I was instantly caught off balance and lurched into her arms. I was in tears of relief and satisfaction. My aunt and uncle were beaming and applauding. Sue C was very pleased. Sue Foyster appeared and was fairly unmoved.

Even in my exhilaration it suddenly dawned on me that this scenario was probably a portent of the future.

During the next week I made several more sorties on the crutches. I learned to walk unassisted, but Sue C followed just behind me for safety. It was twelve yards from my bed to the TV room. I was warmly congratulated by one of the best physiotherapists I have ever worked with.

So I came to the goodbyes, which I am not very good at, even in better circumstances. To the massaging foot nurse who resolutely assured me that if I ever succeeded in taking my life again, she would hunt out my grave and curse it. To M and Kevin, to Ben an older patient who I had recently taken to visiting in my wheelchair, to Janet the talkative cleaner and especially to Mildred, although I hoped the latter would only be an au revoir, as my scrabble partner might well be following on to Mundesley for some convalescence as well. After all I had to get a chance to win at least one game.

The last day on Brooke Ward was upon me. I bought the largest tin of chocolates and toffees dad could lay his hands on, as a totally inadequate gesture of thanks to all the angels in uniform. During the whole of my stay I had received first class attention from cleaner to doctor, consideration and support in every sense, as had my parents.

I had hardly witnessed even a cross word between the highly pressurised nurses and Sister Wake. I simply did not have the words to thank Sue Christie enough, but promised to return one day with a progress report.

As the ambulance men arrived to ferry me to Mundesley I was in for one last surprise. Six of the nurses formed a guard of honour in the ward corridor. I was ushered into a specially prepared wheelchair sprinkled with hospital talcum powder and festooned with streamers and a good luck message.

The girls all sang 'We'll meet again'. I could hardly hold back the tears. One of them kissed me goodbye. Recovering my composure somewhat, I decided that I was onto a winner and kissed them all.

'This must be a popular fellow' remarked one of the ambulance men, slightly taken aback. I felt another slice of guilt fall away from my still chipped soul. This was me, Steve, who none of these nurses had known until I had unsuccessfully tried to obliterate myself. And I was actually liked, and dare I say somewhat loved by people I had never previously met.

It was Monday August, 6, 1986. Due to hospital regulations I had to be wheeled out into the waiting ambulance and the obligatory summer drizzle. But I knew and now you know that I could have walked out through those doors, as long as there were some arms to catch me lest I fell.

Part 2
They Told Me That I Needed Rehab

Chapter 8
Show Me The Way To Go Home

'I sometimes find that when you are faced with an impossible task, it's better to aim that little bit higher' – Steve Foyster

Unfortunately the bonhomie of the departure did not prevail long into the 30-mile 'bumpathon' to Mundesley by the sea.

A few minutes outside Norwich one of the ambulance team enquired how I had obtained my injuries. Feeling buoyed up by the Vera Lynnesque send off, I answered him straight. I do not think he knew how to respond, nor his colleague. So a conversational breaking silence, that stretched about as far as Greenland's tundra, engulfed the remaining miles.

My feeling of guilt for that hour stretched way beyond four letters to an imagined lifetime of pain, misunderstanding and rejection. The ambulance men seemed perfectly happy chatting among themselves. Perhaps I was being hypersensitive. Maybe I just wanted to prolong the 'isn't Steve still a wonderful chap despite what he has done to himself ', thought process for the rest of my days.

To be honest I had not even embarked on a healing process, which is only possible when you start to accept yourself as you are, rather than what you would like to aspire to, physically, emotionally and spiritually.

I have always found a lack of communication most frustrating and hurtful. Many, many things went unsaid throughout my upbringing, however loving the actions were. Honest communication gives firm boundaries, security and trust. I had rather people broke down in tears or screamed vitriol at me, than fall short on the words.

I could not read between the lines with these two, especially as I was wheelchair bound behind their seats. I could not gauge any initial body language. I was simply assuming that they considered suicide a taboo area that they did not feel competent to talk about, despite their medical training. I will never know.

So, it was certainly in a subdued mood that I viewed, with further dismay, the drizzle riven fortress-like outline of Mundesley hospital. It was interesting that every time I returned during the next four months I regarded it at worst as OK and at best a whitewashed haven, nestling among the trees. It is strange how your mind can play such circumstantial games.

The insipid rain had abated somewhat as I was wheeled cordially up a ramp and through the main entrance by a kindly porter called Gordon. My gloom started to lift as a the building began to reveal itself in the style of a rather old fashioned hotel.

During my stay, I discovered that it opened in 1899 as the first large centre in England built specifically for the open-air treatment of tuberculosis. My mother had suffered from TB in her younger days.

My accommodation was on the ground floor, Room 12, Felbrigg Ward, named after a local National Trust estate. It was a single, with the original purpose built full-length casement windows that could open outward and give the maximum impact of fresh sea air.

I was initially quite glad of the privacy after the hurly burly of the Norfolk and Norwich. Camaraderie is one thing, but not being able to go for a pee without half the world knowing is quite another.

In a defiant gesture of single mindedness, I had excluded my parents from the trip, deciding that from the moment I left Norwich, Steve Foyster, the great independent person, had arrived. I would stand on my own two feet from the dubious security of a wheelchair.

So once the very pleasant welcoming nurse had departed, I embarked on the 'great unpacking experience'. There was a single bed, evidently manufactured from granite, a Neolithic chest of drawers, wash basin with mirror, inset wardrobe and an 'easy' chair that looked far from it.

It was while trying to wrestle the wheelchair around these unyielding obstacles, that I started to visualise how tiresome and frustrating an active life in such a sedentary state would soon become.

Previously I had chosen when and where to use my wheelchair. From now on I would need to be framed by it for 90% of my waking hours. It took me two hours to unpack one large suitcase and bag, carefully placing all the relevant articles into wardrobe and drawers.

If I leaned forward too far, putting undue pressure on the footrests, I simply began to analyse the weft of the threadbare carpet. I started to rise to the challenge.

Above all, I had an overwhelming desire to get on with the rehabilitation that very instant. It was just no good being in limbo. I needed to get on. I needed to replace the loss of my last poignant goodbyes with gainful activity and progress. After all, how could I hope to wheel away from the reality of where I was, to where I desperately dreamt of being, while doing nothing?

If this was a rehabilitation centre, where was all the rehabilitation? I decided to explore. Making the most positive and rapid wheelchair exit I could manage, I headed towards the signs marked physio room and gym.

As I passed my next door neighbour I was greeted with a friendly wave, yet I found it hard to decipher his name. I learned later that it was Gerry and that his slurred speech had been caused by a highly debilitating stroke.

Everywhere seemed eerily quiet. Where were all the staff and patients? I peered through locked doors. Lots of soft mats, benches and charts, wall bars and an exercise bike. Yet no people.

Bemused and frustrated I wheeled myself disconsolately back to my room.

At least it was now teatime, which was bound to make things better. Onward and sideways I moved towards the dining room, battling against a wicked camber on the carpeted corridor. This was when I discovered that wheeling a piping hot cup of tea across a large expanse of polished wooden flooring is a fairly hair-raising experience.

What if I was restricted to doing daily tasks in this way for the rest of my life? I started to panic. Then the panic was put aside for another day as it was replaced by feeling terribly alone. I half wished that I had asked my parents to accompany me. You do not always want them around, but where are they when you need them?

The kitchen staff and fellow patients all seemed very friendly, even if the latter were in rather the archive age range. It was simply that I could not face starting all over again and revealing the cause of my disabilities. This was more than loneliness, it was raw-nerved insecurity. I turned my back on the domesticity of the dining room to seek refuge in the solitude of room 12, where I howled my eyes out.

Feeling slightly better I telephoned my parents from the public call box. My feelings of separateness surfaced during the conversation, causing me to lapse into melancholy. There was nothing to do. I hated the place already. I was a 29 year-old boarding school boy on his first day.

My parents placated me, advising me to give it time. They said they would call the ward sister. To my mind she would no doubt be the equivalent of a boarding school matron.

In retrospect I realised that my reaction was understandable. I was facing the unknown, the challenge to walk again. The support network that I had only just left behind had been truly wonderful. I had yet to meet any of my new support team and I had no concept as to how long I would remain on the north Norfolk coast. My parents duly visited late afternoon and also Sue my wife, after I called her in a similar state of distress.

Just before supper there was a knock at my door and Sister Adams entered. It was quite a novelty having staff knock. Even such a small gesture can make you feel more at home. She had the complexion of a peach with a smile to match.

Sister Adams put me instantly at ease, explaining that afternoons were often quiet. Doctor's ward round, which normally took a couple of hours, had been completed late that morning. After that it was free time. She assured me that I would get more than enough time to work out. I was soon to discover that message from Maureen, as I came to call her, was certainly no understatement.

Chapter 9

H is for Heaven?

I awoke next morning in an improved state of mind. Sunshine was streaming between my curtains, certainly a bonus compared to high-rise Brooke Ward.

I managed to wash and shave myself, much to the surprise of the male nurse, Ronnie, who was on call to assist with early morning ablutions. It was nevertheless a tedious, frustrating and at times desperate task, as the pain in my feet was still excruciating. I spent 15 minutes bobbing up and down out of the chair catching glimpses in the mirror, hoping that I was shaving the right bits.

I made a mental note to ask for a hand mirror and started to seriously consider growing a beard, which I had not done for several years. I was beginning to realise that limiting at least some of my expectations, had to become acceptable, if I was to have enough energy left for the fight to walk again.

Mundesley Rehab was so civilised. A nurse brought a cup of tea at 7am. The curtains could even remain closed if so desired, rather than having them ritually thrust open at the crack of dawn. Optional breakfast was taken between 8am and 8.30am.

I am sure that being treated as an individual rather than a named bed, however caring the nursing staff at the Norfolk and Norwich had been, accelerated recovery, or at least the desire to recover for many patients throughout the years.

That afternoon I became acquainted with the gym and was introduced to Bob and Connie, who oversaw the exercise regimes. The physiotherapist who had been allocated to my case was away on a course, so Bob, an affable Welshman nearing retirement, strapped my legs into the stirrups of some hefty springs and left me to try some resistance work.

The muscles were especially weak throughout my right leg. Upon his return I proudly announced that I had completed 200 pulls.

'Two hundred', exclaimed Bob, 'this guy obviously means business. You are going to get on splendidly with H.'

I was so chuffed that I did not even enquire as to the identity of the mysterious H.

Someone high up maybe, a bit like M? Never mind, I was on my way to physical fitness and that was all that mattered to me

The persona of H was revealed a couple of days later. A trim young woman walked into the gym with a purposeful spring to her step and cut the air with a millstone grit accent. Half-a-dozen of the more able patients were than introduced to the infamous 'H training circuit', which included up to 10 gruelling activities, featuring press ups, sit ups, wall-bar work, bench presses and static bike work. After only half-an-hour of this I realised that H certainly meant business.

When I had finally collapsed, H took me aside to record some introductory case notes. She empathised somewhat with part of my emotional trauma and had quite a gentle sense of humour, pointing out that concrete does not offer the most bouncy surface for a high rise fall. I warmed to her style. She asked about the injuries.

'Sprung pelvis that has been virtually pulled back together, compacted lumbar vertebrae, smashed up left ankle and a right leg that is completely useless,' I proclaimed emphatically.

'No such thing as completely useless,' retorted H, somewhat indignantly.

I was yet to be convinced about an appendage that made a wet lettuce look like a stick of celery.

'Up you pop on the bench and we will do a muscle chart.'

Her phraseology was already lightening my mood. H explained that muscle movement/reaction was graded between 4 (fully active) and 0 (almost useless). The left leg performed very well (as a ballet critic might observe), with mainly fours and threes, but only a one for the foot and ankle, which was a bit of a downer for the uppers.

The right leg really struggled. I had no feeling at all below the knee and no voluntary movement in the dropped foot. Above the knee the muscles were very wasted. This was as a result of spending so many weeks prone in traction or dangling from the seat of a wheelchair.

Even H's robust enthusiasm was starting to wane . 'I can't really give that a 1,' she admitted rather deflated.

'Let's try flexing the thigh once more'.

As I tried my utmost, H laid her hand very gently just above my right knee.

'I felt a twitch!' she exclaimed.

'Do it again'.

I complied.

'I can give it ½,' she announced triumphantly.

'We can do a lot with a ½.'

Those words were indeed music to my ears.

'I am leaving for another job in about a month,' H explained, almost apologetically, having just raised my hopes so high.

'But we will do three months work in those four weeks.'

I had the feeling that she was not joking.

I started to pick up vibes that H's reputation for working more intensely with younger patients was not always best received. Her argument was that it was more fruitful to spend quality time with people who had their whole lives ahead of them. I witnessed her spend hours diligently encouraging a teenage girl to try to walk again.

So, she ended up spending an extra half-hour with me every week day and I suppose a bit of the guilt factor started to rear its head again. That particular dragon had to be banished to its lair as we pursued the grail - my mobility.

Occasionally it did cross my mind that H was just a sadist, who had walked into Mundesley Hospital one day, donned a white T-shirt and navy trousers and disguised herself as a physiotherapist. I had heard rumours that she kept a whip in her office to 'encourage' the slackers.

One particular exercise, which I had to endure, involved raising both legs to about 30 degrees above the horizontal off the bench that I was lying on. I had to hold both legs perfectly straight, while H recited, deliberately and almost maliciously, 'Ten Green Bottles'.

By about seven green bottles, I was almost throwing up, my back felt as if a bed of nails was pushing through it and my legs must have weighed about a quarter of a ton.

'Don't let them drop,' H would scream.

I once challenged her about the legendary whip and was aghast when she produced a specimen that Indiana Jones would have been proud of.

I tried to accelerate my independence. I quite upset Ronnie for abruptly refusing his help with putting on my socks first during the morning routine, even though it took a feat of contortion (no pun intended) to carry out this supposedly simple task. I still struggle with the right one.

The pelvis was incredibly sore and the right leg so unresponsive. However, it was good old Ronnie who came swiftly to my aid when I fell completely backwards early one morning, en route to the communal toilets opposite my room.

I had been trying to stagger before I could stumble, using crutches instead of the chair, with a sock on one foot and a slippery drop foot splint on the other.

'You need to take more care beauty,' was Ronnie's gentle advice.

My vulnerability was demonstrated further during an afternoon session when H willed me to walk just one step unaided by crutches. My foot froze. I started to sweat. I simply dared not move, even though my trusted physio was standing within fingertip reach. H reluctantly handed back the crutches, so I could lower myself onto a much-needed chair.

We still had a long way to go, the clock was ticking and time stops for no man or woman.

Chapter 10
Red and Black Letter Days

Although I had settled into the timetable of exercises, physio and occupational therapy, I was not really mixing socially, except at meal times, when I needed the calorific intake to prepare for another high octane session.

The meals were exceptionally good and quite formidable. Cereal, optional cooked breakfast and toast with tea or coffee, mid-morning coffee and biscuit, two-course lunch, mid-afternoon tea and cake, two-course supper and hot drink before bed.

I expressed a real need to spend the weekend with my parents. They were somewhat taken aback and naturally concerned. There was no downstairs toilet in their house and I could not manage stairs. There was no wheelchair access to the back garden and it was still summer, with some really fine weather to enjoy. At least I could wheel myself out of Room 12 to survey the acres and acres of glorious grounds surrounding the hospital, whenever I wanted. It was not unusual to view pheasants or squirrels from my window.

Nevertheless, after due deliberation, they became convinced that it was what I urgently desired and decided to give it a go. Dad would rig up some wheelchair access and purchase a plastic bedpan. It was going to be a really wild weekend.

On the Friday afternoon I was raring to get going. My only concern was that once I had returned to my base in Norwich (that not so long ago I had considered as a place I no longer knew), I might not want to come back. Despite all my commitment to the work ethic during my first few days I had not even bothered to make an acquaintance. We were just about to commence the 'getting the wheelchair into the car' rigmarole, when two porters passed us bearing the luggage of a fresh admission.

'Where is Mrs Miles going?' one of them questioned his colleague.

'Mrs Miles. Do you mean Mrs Mildred Miles' I asked quite agog.

' Yes, that is right. Do you know her?'

Did I know her? Mildred had arrived. My friend Mildred had arrived. This put a whole new complexion on my return after the weekend away.

I literally 'hurtled' up to Mildred's room, and came the closest to a wheelie so far, as I raced across the parquet dining room floor, wrestled open the trellised metal doors of the decrepit lift and finally arrived on the first floor. Mildred was as delighted to see me, as I her. I apologised for having to dash straight off, whilst expressing my delight at having my scrabble arch-rival to share our good and bad times.

We pencilled in a 'seven letter quest' for Sunday evening. Another opportune coincidence some might say. It might have seemed a small thing but it meant everything to me at that stage of my recovery.

Even Christ sometimes had small things to hang onto, a warm stable at birth and supportive words at crucifixion. Small kindnesses can momentarily transform despair into hope and I never cease to be amazed at their timing.

The weekend passed reasonable well. In a very short space of time my father had constructed a gently sloping ramp to give me access to the back garden via the dining room French Doors.

All that effort, yet I was still reticent to use it. I obstinately preferred to struggle with the elbow crutches. Well, I was not going to be in that chair much longer, was I?

Mind you, the 14 stairs that I had so often run up during my teenage years now looked as insurmountable as the north face of the Eiger, so I had to sleep on a mattress in the lounge. With no downstairs toilet, bad memories resurfaced, as I thought about using a bedpan again.

Athletics was on TV. I could not bear to watch my hero Steve Ovett battling it out with Mr Coe. More memories of the joy of running started to gnaw at my soul, and even more than 30 years on can still do, to a much, much lesser extent.

Then I made the biggest mistake of calling Sue, my wife. We really had nothing to say to each other. Yet for me to acknowledge an unknown future apart from her was still too scary in my present state of vulnerability. I begged for her forgiveness, for all the terrible experiences that I had put her through.

'Look Steve', she replied. 'I have forgiven you and God has obviously forgiven you, so isn't it time that you started to forgive yourself? We will always love each other, it is just that we cannot live together any more.'

The first part of the sentence was soothing, the second a barbed hook.

I simply had to start to reconcile myself to an eternal split, yet I was still so traumatised in every other part of my life, that I could hardly bear to even consider it. I could not sleep. I did not want to sleep. I started to pummel the mattress with my fists, yelling 'it is not fair', over and over again, much to my parents' great concern and possibly the semi-detached neighbours.

I was not receiving counselling, apart from a flying visit from my psychiatrist at Mundesley, summoned via my parents. His opening gambit was, 'well Steve, this is a bit of a disaster.'

Maybe one of his ancestors had tried to stop the band playing on the Titanic?

Kind Keith dutifully called round on Saturday. I relented and used the wheelchair to get into the sun on the garden patio, whereupon I trounced him at 10-card rummy.

I decided to sit at the table on a dining chair for meals. I had not thought about how different it would be from sitting up in bed or in the wheelchair. My bent back was pushed against the ergonomically designed curved chair back. The dining table set was purchased by my parents in the 1960s when such a design was ahead of its time.

During 15 minutes of sweat laden self-inflicted hell, the pain was so intolerable that I barely enjoyed any of the food. Why could not I just succumb to lesser expectations for once? However, that sentiment does not mean you cannot change your outlook on the way you tackle life's challenges. I still had to contemplate such sensible lateral thinking.

By Saturday evening I was eager to return to the north Norfolk coast where I would be 30 miles away from my wife. Maybe absence would make the heart less fonder. I had the game of scrabble to look forward to and more importantly I was beginning to understand that you cannot ever return comfortably to a childhood nest. Mundesley had to become my home for now.

Chapter 11
Sweating Blood

There was obviously a great deal of latent anger within me awaiting to erupt. I managed to reduce the potential lava flow into fairly innocuous trickles, via a number of practical, if not emotional ways.

There was archery, once week in the gym, expertly instructed by Eddie who was head of the physiotherapy team. Real arrows were fired from full-size longbows. It took a great deal of effort to hold the bow ready at full stretch. My now muscular forearm twitched before the release and swished a lot of my tension into the target. I became surprisingly good at it, given that I had only tried the sport once before in my teens.

Gradually I was becoming more convinced, as my father had assured me, that I could do virtually anything from a wheelchair. However I was not content to be in one for most of my waking hours.

Another wonderful avenue for stress relief was wheelchair hockey, played indoors. Actually that description slightly belies the truth, as the two teams did not move about. Members were positioned facing each other at arm's length, either on static chairs or in wheelchairs, with the brakes firmly on. Every alternate person had the same colour full length plastic hockey stick, yellow or red, with a goalkeeper for each colour at either end of the human tunnel.

A sponge ball was used, and once thrown into the centre, all hell broke loose. No prisoners were taken as sticks smashed together, often wrenched out of hands by the sheer force of connection. Hand injuries abounded, especially at the crucial sponge-offs, with the first aid kit emerging at various intervals. Yet nobody minded as the pent up frustrations of old and young alike seared from the soul, down the arm and through the stick, during these 'St Trinians-like' confrontations.

Then there was my major dumping ground for anger, the exercise regime. Several of us regularly participated in an hour's circuit training. It was quite a gruelling experience and reminded me of the Canadian Air Force keep fit manual, that was mouldering on a shelf somewhere at my wife's abode. The regime consisted of 20 press ups, 100 plus sit ups, medicine ball work, bench presses and finally as far as you could go in five minutes while motionless on the static bike.

The bench presses involved holding one end of a wooden bench similar to those once used in school assemblies. The other end was clipped into wall bars at waist height, so that it could pivot. One press consisted of lifting the bench from waist height to above head and back down. I could manage to stand up for this exercise, even though the right ankle still gave me a lot of pain. It felt like the endorphins released in this strenuous exercise actually helped me to keep upright.

During my four-month stay at Mundesley various 'sparring partners' joined me in my quest for ultimate fitness. I am particularly indebted to a very pleasant man called Keith, who needed to strengthen his back. He was quite mindblowing at bench presses. We set up a challenge, to find out what was actually achievable in two minutes. Seventy, 80 and 90 came and went. Then Keith set 105, nearly one per second.

When it came to my turn, I thought the game was up. After 90 seconds my chest was scorching and my arms were close to breaking. But as the clock stopped at two minutes I had pressed 106, such was my overriding determination. Keith was pleased for me, even in 'defeat', a fine example of the team spirit and camaraderie that meant so much to us all along the road to recovery.

It is much more important to set your eyes on the goal and run the race, than to win. I did not know if Keith was a Christian and probably never will.

I do have a problem with the label. Jesus Christ was not a Christian. Indeed if you believe in the Virgin birth, his father was God and his mother conceived by the Holy Spirit, so he was not technically born a Jew, simply brought up in that faith tradition. So a lot of the Old Testament would then become prophetic rather than sometimes concentrating on the lineage of David as listed in the Gospel of Matthew. As Christ himself points out in a mystical way, how could he be born of David when he existed before David was born.

He also dared, almost scandalously, to share the most precious gift of the Holy Spirit with a Samarian woman in the midday sun, having sent his disciples off for sustenance. The centurion he cited as having the greatest faith he had ever witnessed, in the land of Israel, was a hated Roman occupier. Once you tear off the labels from our garments, it is usually easier to see the naked love in people of all beliefs and none.

Workouts in the physio rooms were by no means so physically demanding, but usually required more concentration than the gym circuits. Parallel bar work, half an hour of leg work on the mats, a mini-circuit including sit ups, static bike plus balancing exercises. For example, standing on an 18" circular wooden base, which cut through a large ball, while trying to throw another small ball against a wall.

Needless to say I found the balancing exercises virtually impossible. The left ankle was still giving me grief and the right lower leg and foot had a total lack of sensation.

My attitude varied between, 'what is the point of any of this?' as after nearly four weeks I still could not even take one step unaided, to 'at least I threw a ball once, whilst balancing on that stupid contraption'. It all depended on what sort of day I had experienced.

My hospital notes for late August cited that after gym sessions I had taken to the refuge of my bed several times from early afternoon, using the physical pain as the reason, while I was really wrestling with mental anguish.

However I called Waterstones and was in fine spirits after arranging to work two hours on the till, each Saturday morning, as a trial for returning full time when and if I could.

During the physio sessions two things inspired me, a large hand written notice above one of the exit doors which simply read 'DON'T QUIT!' and the Queen tapes which I often requested to be played as we toiled away. His wonderful renditions of 'We Are the Champions' and 'Don't Stop Me Now' meant so much to me at that stage of working through the pain.

If I ever want to be inspired, I still watch the 20 or so minutes of the simply electric 1985 Live Aid Queen performance. If ever I want to cry, I watch the video of Freddie Mercury's last song, 'These are the Days of our Lives'.

At the end of each physio session I dripped sweat across the floor. Sometimes I could not get my shirt off, it was so drenched. Wendy, one of the physiotherapists, used to quip that 'Steve's leaking again.'

 I realise that when Christ sweated blood in Gethsemane, it was true emotional and spiritual angst. On the physical side I think that is the closest I have ever come to following his example.

Chapter 12
Brothers In Arms Must Sink Or Swim

I had been a resident at Mundesley for nearly a month and was really starting to settle into the lifestyle, if not always enjoying it. It was more like being part of a community than a patient in a hospital. Being on first name terms with all the staff apart from Dr Burrows, who ran the show, certainly broke down barriers from the off. A lot of the staff lived locally, which enhanced the 'village' spirit. I reckoned that a week in this particular rehabilitation centre was worth three anywhere else.

The buildings, nearly a century old, were set in total tranquillity, half a mile from the main road next to a golf course. Where better to embark on a holistic recovery? Looking over dew laden lawns towards the sea is a great way to start yet another hard day's graft. My medical notes reflected this as 'Slept well' was noted 13 times between August 26 and September 12.

As my confidence grew I started to mix with and get to know some of the other boarders. Chris, a lovely lad, whose rich brown eyes could melt anybody's heart, had been heavily disabled down one side of his body, with similar symptoms to a stroke. He did most of his talking through his eyes, his verbal response being usually painfully slow for both the recipient and probably Chris. Ironically the debilitation had been caused by a routine operation going wrong. Consultants often appear 'God-like' but can still make mistakes, just like us mere mortals.

Then there was John, who unbelievably had been the cheery builder at Waterstones. He still appeared remarkably cheerful, given he was now confined to a wheelchair, due to a possibly incurable spinal tumour. However his real anger was demonstrated when exercising with the heaviest medicine ball. He bounced it so hard that it regularly hit the gym ceiling, not quite bringing down the polystyrene tiles, just a few flakes.

Peter, a Norfolk man through and through had developed Multiple Sclerosis. He loved listening to Dire Straits. His favourite album was Brothers in Arms, quite apt for our circumstances. Mike, a lovely sandy haired guy, whose boyishness belied his 50 odd years, was suffering from the vestiges of a stroke.

We often used Peter's room as a meeting place between gym, physio and occupational therapy, trying to acknowledge the realities of our disabilities, while fantasising that the situation was merely temporary, like recovering from a particularly bad hangover. We shared the common bonds of fear, expectation, hope and sadness, not to mention the frustration.

I wonder how Christ would have dealt with it all if he had dropped by Peter's room for coffee. Would he have cast out our demons, laid on hands or simply pointed at his wounds and said, 'Well look what I had to deal with. Yet whatever happens, I will be with you until the end of time, even if you are not aware of me.'

Yet frustration and a feeling of hopelessness for the future still led to depressive spells, usually when on weekend leave to be honest, as I shut myself away in a bedroom at my parents.

My nursing notes on Sunday, September 14 stated that this attitude was also bringing my dad down, which was not my intention, it was just my state of mind.

I worked as usual during the morning, after which Keith had very kindly taken me and my wheelchair to a home game at Carrow Road where Norwich City unfortunately lost 1-3 loss to Watford. This had not raised my spirits!

I had visited Sue's parents that evening as well for a regular word card game, which we had played as a foursome for years. It was a bizarre situation really. I knew in my heart that Sue wanted a permanent separation, yet I was catching a glimpse of what were better times, but not to be continued.

To echo the words John Cleese uttered in the film Clockwise slumped on the roadside verge dressed as a monk, with his only means of transport disappearing over the horizon, I could stand the despair, it was the glimmer of hope that I found unbearable.

At least while in the gym, physio room and during occupational therapy I felt I was making progress, even though I did not know to where. After only a week at the rehabilitation centre, Dr Burrows had pronounced that I should use elbow crutches on a regular basis, whenever I felt strong enough, reverting to the wheelchair for rest when required.

My daily aim was to use the crutches from my room to occupational therapy, a distance of about 40 metres. I always had to stop at least twice en route, sitting down on strategically positioned benches, put there for patient rest.

By the time I had reached my goal, I often collapsed onto the waiting stool prepared by one of the occupational therapists. The acute pain in both feet and my back after such a trek almost made me vomit. It took me fully five minutes every time to gain enough composure to relax at all.

Only regular doses of strong painkillers touched the ache, along with friction rubs to the sacro-iliac bones, administered by Sarah the senior physiotherapist. We tried everything else: heat pads, massage pads, even a whole bucket of ice for my right foot, a one-off experience that nearly drew out all my fillings.

Sometimes I simply took to my bed, the ideal emotional escape, where I comfort ate on spoils from the Mundesley tuck shop: lemonade and whole bars of chocolate, complimenting the three huge main meals I was already consuming. Fortunately most of the time the rigid exercise regime kept my weight stable, but it gave me an insight into how eating disorders can easily develop.

Spending more time in bed aroused another frustration. I had been celibate for many months. In the Norfolk and Norwich the catheter had been my personal turn off kit. Even with that removed I think my brain rarely acknowledged that my libido could still function. Although reasonably virile, even in my wildest youth I rarely contemplated sex for the ten times an hour average. If that statistic was proven, no wonder our trains never run on time, and think of all those long sermons.

Now it seemed that my rites of spring were finally surfacing during an Indian summer. Maybe it had something to do with me becoming a man again, rather than just a broken body; a reaction to my consultant's prognosis that I might never be able to have children. My medication often brought vivid erotic dreams, yet I still managed to resist masturbation, as I did not feel comfortable with pursuing it in a bed that was not my own and would be used by someone else upon my discharge.

I could usually manage to reduce my ardour by trying to recall every football team in the English and Scottish leagues. Years later someone tried to provoke me with the concept of Jesus Christ getting an erection. Surely I should regard that idea as a form of blasphemy? Some time after this I heard a woman priest expound on the sensuousness of a prostitute caressing the son of man's feet with her hair and washing them with her tears.

Unless he was created asexual, or completely exhausted at the time, no doubt he would have been aroused to some extent. Yet as a man he evidently chose not to pursue the situation sexually, instead, he used it as an example of self-giving love and to rebuke Peter, one of his closest friends, for not welcoming him into his house with the same level of love, yet not necessarily in the same way.

Restriction reigned in other ways. There was a full size snooker table on the first floor, but it was just too high to play properly from the wheelchair and the pain when I tried to stand for shots was too much for me to concentrate.

I was somewhat dismayed. Again I started to question the so-called divine reward system, which Sue had on one occasion many years ago told me to dismiss. I had reluctantly given up all hope of football and tennis.

One evening both Keith and Matthew, another friend since high school, turned up separately and we swiftly decided upon a game of doubles, John being the fourth player. It was a lot of fun and we all played some good shots, although I was exhausted with the effort and pain by the end. These days when I regularly lose frames against Matthew, during our monthly skirmishes on the baize, my disappointment is often tempered by the memory of how difficult that one frame was.

Everything is indeed relative and sometimes that potentially restricting theory eventually becomes a positive reality.

The weekly swimming excursion to the Cromer Country Club pool, which the centre hired for an hour or so a week, was rather nightmarish. For a start the stone steps leading out of the changing rooms had only one handrail, and were very slippery. I generally had to crawl down these on my backside. Once poolside I had to enter the water by slipping over the edge, as my left ankle couldn't take the the strain of the ladder steps and my right leg and foot couldn't feel much at all.

Of course, once in the water everything became a piece of cake, in fact rather like a sponge. I still could not swim and clung to the edge like a petrified limpet, watching enviously as fellow patients enjoyed a dolphin-like luxury of a few lengths before lunch.

Although Eddie's stalwart efforts with buoyancy aids and eventually hanging onto my trunks as I flailed about came to precious little, just being in water again felt and did me good. So much pressure was released from my much abused feet. Before I left Mundesley I was able to participate in the occasional game of water volley-ball, albeit from the shallow end. I felt included, even though almost out of my depth.

Steve's paternal Grandmother and Grandfather, Ethel and William Foyster

Steve's parents, Roy and Doreen Foyster

The pond at the old Norfolk and Norwich Hospital visited by Steve on a memorable early outing in a wheelchair (see p.42). Photograph, Paul Dickson

Mundesley Hospital. Photograph David Baker Photography

Chapter 13
Autumn Days

As the time came for H to leave, a depressive fug fell over me. How would I be able to continue the battle without my closest ally? But that's life. 'Ol' Blue Eyes' put it very well.

My parents and I said our official goodbyes to H, which sounds very regal, at the Friends of Mundesley Hospital fete. Proceeds from the fete went to the running of the centre. One thing did make me smile though. All week the staff had been bragging about how it had been fine for this annual event for the past decade. Just as the last tombola stall was set up, with the final bottle of sweet sherry displaying its pink winning ticket, down came the rain and everything had to be transferred indoors. We still had a lot of fun revising the methods, rather like that game of snooker.

The next morning I was wonderfully surprised when H came to my room for a short private goodbye. She gave me a list of all the exercises I had to do and at the bottom was a message that inspired me for months ahead.

'Dear Steve, I honestly believe that from now on whatever you want to achieve you will achieve.' Best wishes, Love H.

I have lost the original piece of paper, but I willl never forget that amazing vote of confidence.

Her note caused me to remember a Mundseley minibus excursion to North Walsham for our weekly 'see the outside world experience'. I was sitting next to H in a café, sipping a coffee. It was only about 10 days after my arrival and I was still totally wheelchair bound.

'Do you think I will ever be able to ski? I have never tried before and I have always wanted to,' I asked completely straight faced. I could sense even she was taken aback yet tried to be diplomatic.

'Well I have to say that is extremely unlikely, but I suppose you cannot write it off completely'.

October proved very transitional. H was gone. Of all those who helped me so much along the way, she is the one person I have never been able to contact.

Time moved on and her replacement Rachel arrived. Pleasant enough, but it just was not the same; no Rachel discrimination intended.

Sue suddenly stopped her weekly evening visits. It was always a bit of a charade anyway, as she refused to meet me without both her parents being present. I did not have a chain-saw in the wardrobe, honestly. I asked if I might continue to see her at her parents when I was back in Norwich for the weekend. She agreed with marked reservations. I knew deep down that she just wanted to close me off as a chapter in her life, but I still needed a bit more time to make that emotional adjustment.

Loyal Keith continued to turn up on a weekly basis, either in the virtually knackered minibus, which he borrowed from the secondary school where he was a lab technician, or else on his totally knackered Bantam motorcycle. I used to smirk as I heard a biscuit tin of rusty nails misfiring up the drive, closely followed by an oily, windswept Keith announcing:

'I need an effing fag.'

His demeanour did not improve when I had to explain that given that it was a wooden building, he would have to partake outside. We chatted, played cards or scrabble. He was a continuum in my rapidly changing world.

Mildred was scrabbling back to her home in Ely. Following hip operations she appeared to be suffering a similar sort of pain to me, wincing as she struggled bravely down the corridors, with only sticks to aid her faltering progress.

I sometimes just wanted to pick her up and carry her the last bit but I, of course, was in a similar predicament. It would be like the photographs you see of World War I wounded leading each other, hands on shoulders, not such a merry dance. I promised her solemnly that I would visit once I had fully utilised the amazing free therapy on offer at what was now my main home.

Nevertheless, the real highlight of the month occurred in the physio room one dreary Thursday afternoon, when, given that it was now a truly Indian summer, we were unusually confined indoors for all our exercises. Sometimes there were walking techniques on the terrace, or games on the lawn, but not today.

A heavily pregnant Wendy was putting us through an extra set of leg and feet stretching exercises, when she literally shrieked 'Your toe moved Steve.'

Well my first reaction was wariness of a possible premature birth, and my second was, big deal. I could move five of my toes very well thank you. Wendy sensed my bewilderment.

'No, Steve, your right foot. Your RIGHT foot.'

My right foot? No, it couldn't be. I could still feel virtually nothing below the knee and Sue Christie had said it might take years for the nerve to mend.

'Do it again,' Wendy insisted, leaping down to view my big piggy at close quarters.

And indeed, as I flexed my right foot away from me, the toe moved, ever so slightly. Goodness knows how Wendy even spotted it, but she had, and in a mood of jubilation I telephoned my parents and proudly announced:

'What ho. My big toe moved.'

A small step for mankind maybe, yet an unbelievably big one for me.

We were enjoying the most marvellous autumnal weather. I think the balminess drove some of us barmy. I remember one glorious sunny afternoon when the physio session moved to the lawn. Members of a small group were throwing a football to each other. Suddenly it became a relentless throw the ball at people, with John, Wendy and Mike becoming quite hysterical with contagious laughter. Mike and John chased across the verdant green like two overzealous Long John Silvers trying to claim the treasure of an inflated plastic sphere.

I was jealous of their ability to run, however stutteringly. I also pondered that we were encompassed in a completely different world. We could be on a different planet, or in an artist's scene come to life. I seriously wondered if I would ever be able to fully adjust to the real world again, and how soon that might be.

During boring days we held indoor 'chariot races'. A fairly able-bodied soul, such as Mike or John would push a chair bound charioteer, such as myself or Peter. We would see who could get back from the dining room to our adjacent rooms first.

During one such run things went slightly awry. Three wheelchairs locked together as we entered a chicane. I was in front, careering straight into a door directly opposite nursing officer Stone's office.

Mercifully it was vacant.

About this time, an interesting character who we nicknamed ' Bowthorpe', entered stage right. His nickname came from the part of Norwich that he hailed from.

I still, for the life of me, cannot recall his real name. He had two main interests: not losing at snooker - we witnessed balls fly off the baize in all directions during his fits of pique - and food.

Bowthorpe would be past the first course and well into second helpings of the main before the rest of us were halfway through our vegetables. He ate voraciously, but was still remarkably wiry. I remember on one occasion Peter was eating particularly slowly. One of the kitchen staff came over with second helpings.

'Aren't you going to eat that up?' she challenged.

'Well I would,' Peter replied, with a twinkle in his eye. 'But every time I lift some to my mouth Bowthorpe growls at me.'

It was across the dining room that one Friday evening I spied a female patient of about my age. I was initially attracted to her hair. I have a bit of a thing about hair and her's fell down nearly to the waist. It was still damp, presumably from washing.

I felt no guilt at this attraction. My wife wanted out and although we were not yet officially divorced I had strong suspicions that Sue was already with someone else.

We were introduced the next morning. Several patients had gathered outside the main door, sitting on the benches, some enjoying a smoke in the sunshine. Inevitably someone asked how I had received my injuries, so I replied with the truth. He turned to the long-haired girl who was just out of earshot and pronounced.

'You will never guess what this guy did. Didn't just go and throw himself off a car-park.'

I winced, not solely because such a raw statement brought home the irresponsibility of my actions, but I was also wondering what the newcomer's reaction would be, as she inhaled deeply on her cigarette.

'Well that was a bit silly,' was all that she said, which instantly endeared her to me.

So Julie and I spent the next few weeks sharing some time together. She also enjoyed scrabble, which was a bonus now that triple score Mildred had left, especially as I occasionally won.

Julie was a very dedicated nurse, sometimes caring for severely premature babies at the Norfolk and Norwich Hospital maternity department. We shared our hopes and sorrows. She had become highly distressed at the possibility of having to give up her profession completely, due to a severe back problem. She was also an active member of a church house group at Holy Trinity in Norwich.

Our friendship helped to rekindle my interest in God, the universe and all that I had put on the back burner. I attended the Sunday morning hospital service, but I found the creed very dry. The fellowship, however, was welcoming, which surely mattered much more than the words drawn up by some committee nearly 1700 years ago.

Julie instigated take away runs when two of us went by taxi to the local Chinese restaurant. These evening soirées became a weekly event and, for the first time, I chose not to return to Norwich for the weekend. Mundesley Rehab afforded its patients such an easy-going way of life, as long as they did not abuse the privileges.

Julie's lovely friend Alison drove all three of us to Cromer to partake of lunch in a cosy restaurant. It was a great re-introduction to the normality of the outside world. I even purchased a pair of trousers from a nearby outfitters, which despite the immense effort of sitting and standing many times whilst trying them on, gave me a great sensation of independence.

Our relationship remained platonic although I was slightly tempted after one late night game of cards when I was still in Julie's room situated in the annexe. I was locked out of the main building and could not access Room 12. I nearly resorted to trying to crawl through a window into the main block, but in the end plumped for the embarrassment of ringing the night porter's bell.

Why does everything sound three times as loud at night? Of course the porter kindly passed on the information that I had been locked out in Julie's room after midnight to enliven conversation at breakfast the next morning.

So, it was as close friends that Julie and I parted company, her back somewhat strengthened as she headed Norwich-ward. I promised to give Trinity a whirl when I also made that journey.

Chapter 14
People Who Need People

November 2 was my 30th birthday and I had a unique treat. From the ages of 15 to 18 I had hardly every missed a Norwich City home game, usually accompanied by Keith and his dad, Ray.

The three of us had also been on several away trips, including three Wembley visits, the last one versus Sunderland in 1985, labelled the 'friendly final' as both sets of supporters mixed congenially with each other before and after the game.

Even though City won by a flukey goal, with a deflection from a free kick, the atmosphere of that match lingered long in my memory, especially meaningful to me, given that it was only few months later that my depression started to kick in.

Ray had suggested out of the blue that we should take the pilgrimage to Anfield to see the yellows take on the reds. The game fell on my birthday. I was totally taken aback, given that my usual excursions were restricted to North Walsham, Cromer, or the local take away.

Maybe the 250 miles to the 'hallowed' turf was asking a bit too much for my back. Nevertheless I trusted Ray implicitly. I agreed. We had to leave at six in the morning, so I was up by five, imbibing a nice cuppa that the night nurses had kindly laid on for me.

Poor Ray was slightly late as he had been taken ill in the night and had to stop en route to be sick. But he was determined to drive us. He felt much better after his roadside café grill, a couple of hours into the journey. We had to pick up Keith from Wakefield, where he lived with his girlfriend. Then it was all points west to Liverpool.

We had three brilliant seats with perfect wheelchair access. Although we were thrashed 6-2 - 4-1 down before they brought on Dalglish in the final quarter - the atmosphere was mesmeric, with the roar of 'You'll Never Walk Alone' from a still all standing Kop echoing around the ground. Who could deny these fanatical supporters their own brand of faith, we mused, as we passed street after street of back-to-back terraced houses and boarded-up shops.

We overnighted at a local hotel. The next morning the skies were so clear that we decided to stop off in the Peak District on the way home. The smoky blue Pennines were simply breathtaking. Visibility must have run to 50 miles.

Ray and Keith wanted to have a drink at a hotel in Buxton. I hesitated slightly, but agreed. A great wave of nostalgia started to well up from my gut, through my throat and into a reservoir of a squelchy headache. Buxton was where Sue and I had spent the best of times, a two-week holiday amongst them. Sitting in the luxurious lounge of the hotel that we had occasionally admired but never thought we could afford to stay in, I was exceedingly grateful for the double Scotch, as I cradled the glass in my hands. A spirit to lay another ghost?

I said nothing to my fellow travellers, but both being sensitive chaps, I am sure they guessed that something was amiss. Yet it was still a fulfilling experience, part of the emotional cleansing that has to be worked through when a relationship is irreconcilably severed, whether it be a spouse, lover, friend, parent or sibling, through separation, divorce or death.

I still had some very dark weekends, which were affected by the various constraints of returning temporarily to a parental home having turned 30, as well as increasing lower back and left ankle pain. After a rigorous week of gym workouts, the pain seemed very pleased to free itself, without the shackles of exercise, combined with a lot of free time for negative thoughts.

However, I did take my clarinet, which I had played since the age of 8, back to the rehab centre to rehearse for the Christmas entertainment evening. My notes show that I even cooked myself lasagne from scratch during an occupational therapy session, finishing off the remainder of the red wine, not included in the ingredients (exclamation mark at the end of that nursing entry I noted).

People can be excessively kind. During the 1980s we were being force fed with doom, gloom, evil and despair via television, mercifully only at breakfast and in the regular evening news bulletins. Of course it is 24-hour coverage today. I find it so refreshing that there were and still are so many individuals and groups, more than willing to share great kindness, for no other reason than to bring a little happiness into other and hopefully, if the balance is right, their own lives.

I tried to use crutches inside the hospital. Around the grounds I still required the 'chariot', which I found very frustrating given its limitations. I could not self-propel across grass and the driveway sloped up towards the golf course, so that even given my muscular arms, that route was very difficult to negotiate.

There was an even steeper slope leading past the kitchens. It must have been 1 in 10 at its most challenging . One afternoon I decided to attack the hill. Starting off quite confidently and swiftly, my eyes were bulging with the strain by the time I passed the kitchen door. I reached the summit coughing and wheezing, almost awaiting the first signs that would need the 'Papworth crew'. I felt as though I should plant a flag.

Janet the senior member of the kitchen staff had witnessed my endeavours. 'I thought it must be you. Why on earth didn't you go the other way?', she wanted to know.

'Oh I thought it would be quicker,' I gasped unconvincingly.

Stuart, a very debonair patient, who reminded me of a Gerald Harper/ Nigel Havers clone, must have also taken in some of my mobility madness. Two days later on a very fine Wednesday afternoon, he offered me a spin in his sports car, an MG if my memory serves me correctly.

I was thrilled. I had only ever once travelled briefly in such a vehicle. I was rather concerned that driving a low cramped machine would not do Stuart's bad back any good, but he brushed this aside. Perhaps it was his act of defiance. The trip was terrific, speeding along narrow country roads, stopping off at North Walsham. I remained mesmerised in the car while Stuart carried out his errands.

On the return leg, he suggested that a visit to the sea would fit the bill. We arrived at Walcott. My enthusiasm for watching the spume of an almost wintry sea cascade against the mad-made wall was clearly evident.

Suddenly Stuart started up the engine. I was disappointed that we were moving on so quickly. I was then astonished as my driver negotiated the concrete slope onto the just wide-enough sea defence. It was almost like being in the water, but not nearly so cold, even with the sea spray swirling about our faces. The memory of this spontaneous act of kindness still makes me tearful - a piece of heaven on earth from an angel in a sports car.

Before H's departure I had repeatedly pestered her to get me back on a bike. Norman Tebbitt would have been proud of me. Unfortunately we ran out of time. Now with Rachel's guiding hand on the saddle, I eventually achieved my goal. It was no mean feat. Owing to the pelvic complications it was difficult to get my leg over the crossbar. My weak right leg meant an inbalance on the pedal pressure. More than once the brutal hardness of the terrace paving slabs loomed to meet my elbows and knees.

My perseverance was rewarded one morning when Sarah, the head physio suggested that she, Rachel and myself should all cycle into town. There was a fair head wind against us on the outward journey. The hospital road seemed to have developed a few hills overnight. I had to dismount a couple of times, but it was almost as arduous dragging the cycle along. However, on the return, with the wind behind me, I freewheeled down the last incline to the hospital and whooping with joy I glimpsed another piece of heaven. Sarah laughed, which on retrospect was quite a fitting biblical analogy.

Chapter 15
Going, Going, Gong

At junior school I was always the goody-goody, top marks in nearly everything, trying so hard to get on with all the teachers. I do not know why. It did not feel like creeping, it just seemed to come naturally.

I remember some things with acute embarrassment, such as when I stayed behind to help a struggling cleaner put all the desks straight. This was mentioned by the form teacher in front of the whole class the next day. Yet I also remember that I was glad that I stood up for a fellow girl pupil against the bullying tactics of our infant school headteacher, again in front of the whole class.

My seemingly saint-like vocation even led my fairly strict junior school headteacher to wish I would do something wrong for once. Curiously enough, I was reasonably popular with a few of my peers, although it was generally me inviting them to my home rather than vice versa. I did however have a piece of English, which had been displayed on the classroom wall, completely smudged out with water, and also the duplicate, which I had painstakingly copied out in fountain pen.

At grammar school it was a completely different ball game. The 'hard nuts', who by the fifth form had abandoned any hope of academic qualifications, became quite adept at trying to injure as many of their fellow pupils, who were trying to get on at school.

Ideal opportunities to carry out disguised physical bullying were found in the mass lunchtime free for all kick-about. Fortunately I became proficient at swerving the tackles. When the bone-crunchers did make contact the culprits felt the full hardness of my shin bones, which served me so well in later times.

I never deliberately retaliated to injure an opponent, but as I played mostly right back or centre half, I could go in very hard. Such tackles, seen as fair then, would probably get me a life-time ban today, together with a fine payable to the local diving school.

I still remember a particularly vicious tackle, outside school, while playing for a youth team on a rainy Sunday afternoon on a muddy pitch in Fakenham, north Norfolk. I honestly thought that my shin bone was broken despite the old fashioned pad, but it was just chipped. It was me who stood up first, my adversary was still writhing in agony on the turf.

Being good at most of my academic subjects at GCE O-level meant that several of my teachers wanted me to take their subjects at A-level. I was quite torn and still regret the decision to take dry mathematics as opposed to juicy English literature, especially as I could not comprehend the maths master's working in the 10th dimension scenarios.

I was a lonely adolescent. My parents bought a dog for company and sometimes I ended up mixing with my brother and his friends who were four years younger.

When I started to date, my parents wanted to know exactly where I was, who I was with and when I would be home. One night I rebelled against this cotton wool constraint, and went on a very heavy drinking spree with Keith, including almost a bottle of gin, which I have never touched since. We played poker at the YMCA until the early hours.

By 4am, Ray and a police officer had managed to track us down. My mother and father were frantic. Despite being sorry, ashamed and repentant the next morning, I still felt as though I had made a statement of rebellion.

Maybe it was partly a desperate effort to finally destroy my apparent goodness that drove me to jump. I am sure that making up for lost naughtiness led me to carry out a hospital prank that unfortunately got rather out of hand.

Another influential person had come into my life at this time. Jill was about my age and had been afflicted by the ruthless Guyon Barre's Disease, which strips down nerve fibres. It was the same condition from which the author Joseph Heller had recently recovered.

The disease had attacked Jill until all but her neck, head and breathing were paralysed. Mercifully she had a remission, but was still completely wheelchair-bound.

Despite all the odds being stacked against her, she had a great sense of humour and we soon became firm friends. She also played a fair game of scrabble, a mean game of crib and we even attempted rather haphazard darts sessions, usually with nobody else in the room as the board was rather difficult to hit. We had a very honest relationship, laying open the most raw of our emotions.

We helped each other along the wheelchair way. I tried to give Jill the will to walk again and she loaned me the back of her chair to lean against as I walked behind her, pushing with all my might to and from the dining room at meal times.

Jill taught me how to foot stretch. Jill gave me back a sense of humour, not always the Basil Fawlty mania that still surfaces from time to time, more the fun of Eric Morecambe. We did silly things to attract attention and wind people up, and were somewhat affectionately labelled 'the Terrible Twins'.

One evening, probably over a glass or two of wine, we started imagining a daring prank, like balancing a traffic cone onto the topmost point of the highest hospital turret. It was all mind games really, yet the next afternoon I had an even better and more practical idea. For some reason a compulsion to carry it through overcame my common sense.

At 6.45 pm, straight after supper, I started to wheel myself purposefully back to my room. As I passed the main foyer, I grabbed the two-foot diameter brass gong, the banging of which announced every meal time. I belted off to secrete it under my bed, just in the nick of time. Mrs Stone emerged from her office, a mere 10 yards away, heading for the dining room, just as I was heading in the opposite direction with the 'stolen goods'.

I sat and waited. Ten minutes later, Jill in wheelchair burst into my room and announced:

'The gong has gone missing. Mrs Stone has ordered the porters to make a full search of all rooms'.

' I know', I replied smugly, 'It is under my bed'.

Jill would not believe me until I lifted up the counterpane to reveal the loot. It was then that I had to decide whether to come clean or not.

'What is the reaction like, apart from Mrs Stone's?', I asked.

'Oh the patients and nurses are lapping it up,' enthused Jill.

Right then, I decided that I would keep this going for a bit longer, but in a full scale search, surely under my bed, in the first room along the corridor, would be the obvious place to look?

Maybe I should double bluff. In the wardrobe, behind my suitcase and hanging clothes would be better. As quickly and quietly as possible, we transferred the treasure from the floor to the new hiding place. There were a couple of heart-stopping bongy moments. Within a few seconds of shutting the wardrobe doors, one of the porters entered my room brandishing a torch.

' You are not hiding a gong in here, are you?', he enquired quite genially.

The ridiculous scene almost caused me to dissolve into helpless mirth. Biting the side of my mouth to gain full facial control I stated quite brazenly:

'Do we look like the sort of people who would steal a gong?'

After a cursory glance around, the would be Sherlock left for the next room and we both fell into fits of laughter.

The hilarity seemed to be infectious as we heard a nurse in the corridor gaily trilling, 'Anybody seen a gong?'

Jill and I tried to remain as natural as possible until lights out, playing scrabble and cards and partaking of the habitual hot drink. Jill eventually left for her room and I contemplated whether I should wait until morning, or act promptly to rectify the situation.

At 11.45pm, I peered outside down towards the hallway. There was nobody around. The night nurses were boiling a kettle and chatting. I could guess one of the topics of conversation.

Stealthily and noiselessly I wheeled myself foot by foot towards the gong hooks. It seemed to take forever, not made any easier by the wicked camber on the carpeted floor, which had already caused many a chariot race to founder.

Suddenly I was at my destination, rehanging the missing object without a sound. I was back to my room in no time, without encountering a soul. Despite my bravado, I was mightily relieved to see my bounty back in its rightful place.

Unfortunately, or possibly fortunately, I had not fully realised the true furore that my impulsive actions had caused. The nurse who brought my early morning tea was full of it.

'Do you know what?' she said.

'No, what?' I replied blearily.

'Last night the gong went missing, and Mrs Stone went crazy. She had the porters out in the grounds for hours with torches and even called in the police.'

Oh God. My heart sank. 'Did they find it?', I asked.

'Oh yes. It mysteriously reappeared this morning.'

I knew that I would be for it. I had to be the prime suspect, given my new found mischievous sense of humour. It was at the breakfast table that the KGB style tap on the shoulder arrived via one of the nurses.

'Mrs Stone would like to see you please.'

It was like a scene from The Wimslow Boy in Mrs Stone's office. Her facial appearance mirrored her name. Would it be the strap, cane or roasting over an open fire?

' Yesterday evening Steven', (at least it wasn't Foyster), 'the hospital gong was removed and I have reason to believe that you had something to do with it. Do you deny this?'

'No, I don't deny it. I took it, but I put it back. It was only meant to be a joke.'

'Well I did not find it very funny. I was here until 10pm sorting things out with the police.'

It was chewing mouth time again. 'But it wasn't money or drugs,' I protested.

'Nonetheless it is quite a valuable item and part of the hospital. I understand you have decided to leave us at Christmas. You are a mature adult and should behave accordingly.'

Why am I being treated like a 10 year-old I wondered, yet dared not express this.

With, 'That will be all,' Mrs Stone finished the interrogation.

I felt reprimanded, yet still triumphant, secretly wishing that my ex-headteacher had witnessed the whole scenario.

So, I had indeed decided to leave my now beloved Mundesley. Following a progress interview with Dr Burrows and other members of staff, during which I was kindly offered more time to grow both physically and mentally stronger, I still felt that having been an inpatient for seven months in two medical institutions, I could not face a new year in the same situation. I decided to pack my bags on December 18, the day that the hospital closed for the festive break.

It was a busy time. Occupational therapy was even more purposeful as I made Christmas presents for all my relations: reed-woven stools, macramé owls etc - the sort of gifts that would probably be received somewhat unenthusiastically.

I just had to pay for the materials, so it was both meaningful and inexpensive. I no longer needed the drop-foot splint and had abandoned my wheelchair for elbow crutches, and on good days, two sticks.

I still had my bad days when I used the pain as an excuse to burrow below my blanket and comfort eat in my bed. On one such occasion, Jill and another patient had to almost drag me physically from the sheets to play a couple of hands of rummy. I was very angry at the time but later was touched that they had cared enough to do so.

I reckoned that I was getting cold feet, and keeping them under the bedclothes improved the situation. It was a much better day when I had my spot playing Stranger on the Shore at the Friends Of Mundesley Hospital concert.

Having practised, it did not sound too bad. Colin who accompanied me on the piano had to wrestle with an instrument that seemed to have more silent keys than a redundant prison, and my bottom F would not function without a squeak. It was hardly Acker Bilk, but even so it was well received, a great confidence booster for me as I had managed to stand for five minutes throughout the whole piece.

I had two meetings with a hospital discharge social worker who was intent on finding me a flat or bedsit in Norwich for the new year, even driving me to a meeting with the council housing officer, a week before my leaving date. He was an affable enough chap but did not seem to be able to relate to what had caused my circumstances and was most keen to chat about wanting to return to his beloved Canadian homeland.

December 18 duly arrived, along with the Christmas lunch, the only meal of the year when staff and patients mixed at the tables. And who should be sitting opposite me but Mrs Stone. What a coincidence. We had not even exchanged eye contact since 'the incident', let alone words, so I did not exactly find the turkey and roasties sliding down with ease.

However, we exchanged pleasantries and the lubricating sherry and wine aided the swallowing and lifted the atmosphere. With the pudding consumed and the coffee served, we were allowed to smoke. Mrs Stone lit up, proffering me one of her cigarettes. She smiled as I accepted.

Forgiveness, the ideal present and another fond memory to cling onto, as later that afternoon I left the centre that had become 'home' and prepared to go boldly where I had gone before, but not as the man I now was. This was not a final frontier, just another bridge, but I had a feeling inside me that some of the wooden slats would be very tricky to cross.

Part Three
The Road to Revelation

Chapter 16
One Stagger Forward

One week to a fairly dreaded Christmas. Why is it that this particular festival is built up so much to be a perfect time?

The nativity story is hardly a good example of 'perfection'; a 70-mile hike for an eight-month plus pregnant girl astride a donkey, a manger for a cot, then a bunch of shepherds and heavenly hosts to contend with, when all the new mother and indeed father needed was some decent kip. If little Lord Jesus no cry did he make, that must surely precede Cana as the first miracle.

Even ignoring the retail hype, if you can ever manage it, family tensions are supposed to be on hold, a bit like the World War I truce. Of course this year I was spouseless, apart from a final evening meet up at Sue's parents before the New Year.

I spent quite a lot of time wrapping macramé owls, but not woven stools as they were rather averse to cheap wrapping paper. I also wrote Christmas cards for family and my new-found friends, Mildred, John, Mike, Jill and M.

Despite the dread, Christmas Day went OK. I enjoyed the lunch, albeit somewhat subdued, determinedly sitting at the dining table. However, the back pain was severe by the end. I seem to remember playing scrabble with my father and being fairly evenly matched. This was the first of many, many such encounters over the next two decades and more.

During the 'festering' period we also watched some videos that I had bought or rented from a local shop. I found Crocodile Dundee amazingly humorous. My father said it was the first time he had heard me laugh in 18 months.

Matthew took me to the morning service at St Peter Mancroft, the very big civic church that he had attended regularly from a choirboy. I found it quite dry. If only I had realised how much that place of worship would be intertwined in my life for the next decade.

I was now managing to walk with a stick and on Boxing Day completed the mile or so rectangle that featured the local library. I had first visited the library as an eight year-old and was astonished that you could borrow books for nothing, with the smell of book and polished wooden floor as an added extra. There was Farrows, one of the best fish and chip shops in Norfolk and the Heartsease public house, where I was first introduced to alcohol through a pint of Guiness aged about 16 (it nearly put me off beer for life). Finally I passed the local Methodist church, which still remains.

I stopped off in the pub, as it was a convenient halfway point. I found it nostalgic in a strangely separated way. When My Song came up on the juke box I found it all a bit too much and finished off the swift half even more swiftly.

Although I spent Christmastide at my parents', I did have the impetus of moving into the cluster unit bedsit room in the New Year and also attempting to return to Waterstones in a phased progression.

The last meet up at my in-laws was very emotional. My wife had transferred most of my belongings, including a small snooker table and wedding photographs, to their garage. At the end of the final evening that we would ever all be together, my father-in-law drove me and seven years of my life back to my parents home. He admitted to being very sad about the situation. We had got on well, always sharing the washing and drying up after the evening meal, and having a joke during the ritual procedure.

I have learnt over the ensuing years that ritual can play a vital part in our lives, as long as it does not become obsessive. Rural and seasonal festivals dating back thousands of years whether pagan, Christian, Jewish, Muslim, Sikh or Hindu, give focal points to the year.

Birthdays and anniversaries are usually anticipated and celebrated, especially round numbers from 30 upwards. Is that influenced by the biblical 'seven score years and ten'?

Of course, if you have been bereaved, separated, or divorced the dates can become very poignant, especially during the early years of loss. It is almost unbearable for some, especially if the loss has been through a tragedy. I had survived what some have said would have been a tragic loss. I should have been eternally grateful, but I was still working through what I had lost and what I was trying to gain.

I was becoming a bit desperate to find a rhythm in my daily life and meaning for my survival. I had found structure helpful in some of the sporadic church services that I had so far attended. Although I found communion at St John's RC Cathedral somewhat tedious, at least it followed a rubric. Sue had encouraged me to go there, even though I had not acquired the necessary church 'stamp'.

I preferred going to Norwich Cathedral evensong, with fewer attendees in a small side chapel. Sunshine often streamed in on a late summer afternoon. There was nearly always a Cathedral Close itinerant called John in attendance, dressed reasonably enough but obviously struggling with mental health issues. He often came out with a few loudish 'Fucks' during the usually very quiet half hour, but the service never stopped and indeed the presiding priest just waited for him to calm down before continuing. Christ with the marginalised being lived out. This struck a chord with me even then.

The Mount Zion services at the church which Bob and Ann attended were full of lively worship, yet seemed a bit of a free for all, depending on who was moved by the Holy Spirit. I would have thought that initially a non-churchgoer like me would be carried along for a while by the uplifting songs and biblically based sermons (albeit usually half-an-hour too long in my opinion), but might eventually be more content with a basic format, especially at the sacramental rituals of weddings and funerals.

January proved to be a bitter month across the United Kingdom, with an average temperature of only 0.8 celsius. Even main A-roads in rural Norfolk were totally blocked and Mundesley Rehab Centre made the national news when they ran out of heating oil and a supply had to be airlifted by helicopter from the Midlands.

Although I sorely missed the camaraderie, at least the thought of icy draughts from the window and door leading to the lawn from Room 12 made me appreciate my parents' centrally heated semi- detached, and likewise the cluster unit into which I moved at the beginning of the next month.

I have to say that the warden and my fellow residents were very convivial. The ground floor room was also convenient for outside access, with a fridge and wash basin. However all cooking facilities were in a communal kitchen up a flight of stairs which I found almost impossible to negotiate with crutches or stick as I clung onto the bannister. There were many days I preferred to make do with bread and cheese or cereals rather than risk the ascent.

My staple cooked diet, when I did make it to base kitchen one, was warmed baked beans or tinned ravioli. Steady consumption of the latter reminded me somewhat sardonically of an episode in the brilliant comedy Rise and Fall of Reginald Perrin, when Reggie ordered it for all three courses in a restaurant. He had just reinvented himself and I was in a similar situation, but hardly comedic.

The next challenge was returning to Waterstones three days a week. It was a pleasant enough walk from flat to shop, with a section by the river. It was only a quarter-mile in total. yet I was totally worn out by the time I arrived at the shop, having to pause every 10 yards or so, using riverside railings for support, and self-consciously pretending to take in the view.

I was exhausted after a seven-hour day and tok a return route that avoided the shadow of St Andrew's car park, even though it was marginally longer. There was a nice cosy wine bar just by the bridge into Coslany Street, which I often frequented just before returning to my little sanctuary. I found my singleness there quite raw and never stopped for more than one small or large glass, dependent on my mood.

I had started writing letters to my fellow travellers from the previous summer. There is always something special about receiving a handwritten epistle, although this is extremely rare today. Email, text, or Facebook communication can hardly compare. I must admit that I am not a great fan of ecards.

A letter takes time to compose, is usually considered and not limited to 280 characters of twittering. I still love the colour and varied designs of real Christmas cards displayed about the lounge.

I remember the trials of wrestling with high school ink wells and fountain pens that were filled by suction before the invention of cartridges. Somehow it was part of another ritual, which often gave me time to think what I was going to write. I was now using speedy ballpoint. At least there would be less chance of blotting my copybook.

M had been transferred to York hospital and discharged in mid- August. He had been delighted that there was a TV in each ward or side room as a diversion . He had received very good one-to-one physio and was due to have an artificial leg fitted at Chapel Allerton hospital in Leeds, which was good news, as in his words 'hopping about using a walking frame is knocking hell out of me'.

Mildred had been at Mundesley at the same time as me for rehabilitation following a hip operation which, to her bitter disappointment, had proved unsuccessful. However during early 1987 she was admitted to the RAF Hospital in Ely for a Stanmore hip replacement which she hoped 'would see her out'. Thankfully I received a much more positive response to my Easter card and letter.

Mike, back in Lincolnshire, had been told by his doctor that it would be a long time before he could consider work and, although he enjoyed discovering new books and music, he felt that his life remained dormant.

I had a similar downer to Mildred at my follow up appointment in February with my consultant. Although he was very pleased with my progress,he was not considering any medium term surgery on either my lower back or left ankle. They were both causing me the most distress, even with a staple diet of co-codomal, the only painkiller that soothed at the time. I also had a back belt support, which I had acquired at Mundesley, which helped to alleviate the pain once upright.

 I was referred to a supplier of surgical footwear and trusses - well I needed all the support I could get. It was a charming establishment in an Edwardian building in Upper St Giles, Norwich. I have to admit that I had a rather ageist attitude on my first visit. What was a young man like me doing in a place for the elderly and infirm? That mindset was totally reversed in the years to come.

 It was a bit like a scene out of the sitcom Are You Being Served, with the middle-aged male footwear technicians complete with tape measures and a wooden counter. It was here that I first encountered Derek Hayter, a very pleasant, caring man with a twinkle in his eye, who became my allocated foot specialist for many years. The boot measurements were completely different as my right ankle and forefoot already had a lot of calcification. This meant that the lengths and especially widths, taken on sketch drawings, or standing barefoot on greaseproof paper, had to be very accurate.

Dealing with another human being's feet is a very sensitive occupation, bordering on a vocation, especially during the initial contact. Feet are so important. They are in use for the larger part of the day, even when sitting.

The disciples of Jesus walked many, many miles over dry and rough terrain. So, it comes as no surprise, however scandalous Peter thought of the action, that the human Christ washed their feet and that the woman with the alabaster jar washed Christ's, this time to the horror of his host Simon the Pharisee.

My New Year message comprised a decree nisi confirmation letter, advising me that I would need to attend a meeting at the relevant solicitor to agree to the decree absolute and the terms of the divorce. I had not expected it so soon. It is always a bit of a shock to see endings in black and white. There had been issues on both sides during our seven year marriage, yet au revoirs are one thing, final goodbyes are another.

The solicitor was very pleasant and during the meeting, noticing that I was becoming a little emotional, she commented that it appeared that I did not really want the divorce. I concurred but confirmed I that I would not contest it. Sue had been through enough during the past two years. The financial agreement was reached amicably enough. Sue kept the bungalow and I received half of the value via a cheque.

At least I had financial security. I was hopeful that I could still drive, as this would greatly increase my independence. I was still relying on lifts from dad, or cycling very locally.

I remember my first venture across Mousehold Heath, accessed close to my parents' house, to have tea with some acquaintances who were conveniently based about a mile or so away on the other side of the heath. I did not fall off, but was completely shattered and seem to remember dad picked me up with the velocipede for the return visit.

I tried out an adult tricycle, which someone local wanted to sell. I rode it within the confines of the parental home's cul-de-sac and found it exceptionally cumbersome and unwieldy to turn. I felt a bit of a failure and so was very pleased to learn over 30 years later that Matthew, who rode every type of cycle from penny farthing to tandem and Brompton folding bike, had experienced similar issues.

Cajoled by Matthew, I had started attending the 10am service at St Peter Mancroft. They had three excellent regular organists and a very good choir, boys only of course. With often well over 100 members in the congregation, the music was still able to fill a church that could easily seat more than 500.

Sadly, I really started to struggle at Waterstones. Sitting upright on the till played havoc with my lower back, leading to lack of concentration and fairly regular days of sick. It came as no surprise at the end of February, that the two managers and me arrived at a mutual agreement that I could no longer continue working there.

At least I was able to say some proper goodbyes to my fellow booksellers this time, rather than hurtling out of the main door towards the nearest multistorey.

Chapter 17
Reverting to Type?

I continued to worship at St Peter Mancroft. During one of the after-service coffee get togethers, Matthew introduced me to David Bradford, a long-standing city councillor who had been wheelchair-bound for most of his life due to childhood polio. We talked about mobility and my desire to drive a car again and improve my independence.

Due to the severe weakness of his legs, David used a car adapted with hand controls for brake and accelerator. He very kindly offered to let me do a test drive. Strangely I had walked past his specially adapted bungalow hundreds of times as a schoolboy, taking a cut through from the nearest bus stop to my parental home. I also saw his children return home from time to time, unaware who their father was.

So I caught the same bus, albeit with a different number and lengthened route, walked through the same cut and received a warm welcome from David and his wife Thelma. Once in the driver's seat I found the controls very alien, having been used to driving a manual car for about six years prior to the jump. I had passed my test first time but not until my mid 20s.

Everything went rather bumpily, yet relatively OK through the quiet cul-de sac and adjoining side roads in the housing estate. However, when we came to a halt at the t-junction to the main road, I somehow moved the hand controls onto accelerate by mistake and we lurched into the middle of the two traffic lanes.

An oncoming motorist travelling from the left slammed on his horn and brakes, not surprisingly gesticulating and mouthing his anger, and missed David's car by about three feet. Mercifully the motorist was able to avoid a head-on collision by swerving into the other lane.

I was extremely shaken and apologised profusely. David seemed fairly unphased and emphasised that nobody had been hurt. He even asked me if I would like to continue. I declined his kind offer, swapped seats and was driven back to my parents for a stiff cup of well-sugared tea.

I started to wonder if I would ever manage to drive again. I had owned a Honda 90 motorcycle in my youth, but did not relish the idea of trying to manipulate such a vehicle in winter conditions, even if my legs and back were capable of doing so safely.

Then the never-let-it-be-said family mantra started to re-echo through my mind. I had driven a manual Volvo during my marriage. My father had bought the same model a few years ago. The Volvo dealer was Holden Motors, so I contacted them wondering if I might be able to drive an automatic, given the multiple fractures of my left ankle and my inability to co-ordinate a steering wheel throttle.

I was still working at Waterstones when David Holden, one of the business brothers, unexpectedly turned up at the shop at the end of a Saturday morning shift. He introduced himself and blithely stated that outside was a very good second hand automatic Volvo hatchback for me to test drive.

After, or maybe because of the initial shock, I followed him to the car and despite my reservations I succeeded in driving us safely the three miles to my parent's house.

I could manage the feel of the accelerator through my newly acquired boots and, I have to admit that despite the nervousness, I was exhilarated to be sitting more confidently behind the wheel. And so it came to pass that I spent a few thousand pounds from the divorce settlement on a metallic blue passport to relative freedom.

I have always loved walking from early days. Maybe the traipsing around with paternal grandmother had instilled it into my soul. However, cycling had always been my favourite method of transport, as I was able to get to maximum speed from a standing start in a small timeframe and could see so much more from the saddle.

If I could travel everywhere by train rather than road I would, but as with many other parts of the country, Norfolk's branch lines were decimated by Dr Beeching. I have never bothered much about models of cars, except for safety or efficiency, unless a reader of this feels he or she is moved to drop a soft top Aston Martin DB6 onto my driveway. Yet to be able to go wherever I wanted, whenever I wanted, by way of an 'infernal combustion engine' was truly momentous for me, as I drove along the winding rural roads.

I still had very dark times, especially with so much time on my hands post-Waterstones . There was also a certain amount of guilt now, as I had left a position for which I received sick pay while being hospitalised.

I remember one sunny Sunday morning when I had skipped church, buried under the duvet with the thin curtains drawn, letting in too much light for my liking. At about midday there was an unobtrusive knock on my door. There was Matthew wondering if I was all right. He had missed me at the service.

'It is a lovely day out here Steve,' he observed .

'Well it might be for you,' I retorted sharply and simply closed the door. I was on a combination of antidepressants that I would continue to take every day for two more years.

I needed to register with another surgery, my official address now being Coslany Street. I rang up the nearby Prince's Street practice and duly made my initial appointment with a Dr John Lofting. I found him to be very attentive, as he listened to a potted version of my recent medical history and gave me over half-an-hour of his valuable time.

I have to say that the other patients looked somewhat miffed as I passed through the now crowded waiting room. But I felt more elated than when sitting behind my Volvo's steering wheel. Someone was finally listening to me.

Dr Lofting not only listened but referred me in two different directions; the first for a steroid injection in the area of my right knee, to hopefully reduce the pain and maybe even increase the mobility. The second was to a course of group therapy sessions, back at the Norvic clinic. So my escape mission must have been rumbled after all.

The injection appointment arrived first, as there was a longer wait for mental health referrals. Sadly that non-parity still exists more than three decades on. The procedure was carried out by Dr Duthie, whose Gaelic sense of humour was mostly reassuring. The injection was via a fairly standard-sized needle but linked to a syringe about a foot long.

'I am just going to give you a wee bit of a medical cocktail,' he explained. 'Should be fine. Same sort of mix which I used to tranquilise elephants in Africa.'

To this day I am not sure how true this was. His assistant also had to reduce the blood flow to my lower leg with a very tightly bound black rubber tourniquet just above the knee. This was so the full strength of the cocktail hit the right spot.

Restricting the blood supply became quite painful, but Dr Duthie reassured me it would need to be released after 15 minutes maximum, or my leg might drop off. Anyway this one-off injection helped a great deal to reduce pain and assisted mobility, especially when driving. The 'tusk force' had completed their mission successfully.

It was strange returning to the Norvic Clinic, even though I had only spent 10 days there the year before, and coming to terms with the fact that I was now an out patient attending group work one day a week.

The group comprised six to eight members, all of whom had suffered quite severe depression or mental trauma. The sessions were led by Dr Julia Clark, a very caring and kind psychologist.

There was an issue, however, that did grate with me. Having found Dr Lofting who listened to me from the start, I was now very keen to talk about my state of mind. Dr Clark liked to give members all the silence that they needed during the two hours, which was broken by lunch at the onsite canteen.

Lots of the members seemed to like this option. I do remember protesting strongly at an early session, after 45 minutes of silent angst. This did not go down too well with some group members. Julia duly calmed the ruffled feathers, including mine, and lunch was served.

After about a month we came to a mutual understanding that this style of group therapy was not the best option for me. I made an appointment with Dr Lofting to discuss an alternative. During the appointment he had to leave the room to talk to someone in reception. My notes were on his desk and at the top was his letter of referral to Dr Duthie. I could not resist a quick scan.

Dr Duthie mentioned me as 'a young man who had made a somewhat miraculous recovery'. I found this a bit disturbing to be honest and very unusual phraseology for a medical communication.

When Dr Lofting returned I felt that I had to mention it. He explained that since he had taken on his practice, four patients had sadly attempted suicide from a multi-storey, only two had survived, including myself, and the other was in a wheelchair for life. I later discovered that John was a regular churchgoer. Maybe Dr Duthie was as well. Still it was a highly unusual statement in an era when science was the new God.

One definition of a miracle is 'an extraordinary and welcome event that is not explicable by natural or scientific laws and therefore attributed to a divine agency'. I suppose my physical recovery could somehow be seen in that context, but I was still struggling big time both mentally and emotionally.

The prayerful power of David Broome's hands on my head remained from time to time. Nevertheless, I think that once you get carried along the 'God's will' route, you can end up in a dangerous one way street and even a very tight cul-de-sac.

Over the years I have wrestled with the 'why did I survive' conundrum, especially after two young people I knew personally, one quite well, took their own lives by jumping, one from the top of a tower block, which gave even less chance of avoiding death.

I have found the phrase 'God has a plan for you', often touted by well-meaning Christians who usually do not even know me, to be at the best trite and at the worst piling on unwanted expectations of potential 'redemption' through good works.

Should I become a healer, a missionary, a soap box evangelist? Two years later, I did realise that during a conversation with a priest who I had only just met, that I was not yet ready to use my experience to benefit others.

Over the years I have experienced what appeared to be divine timing again and again. I have also discovered that to sit in a quiet garden on a sunny afternoon and enjoy a cup of Earl Grey tea, or a glass of good red wine, while silently giving thanks to God and all the people who have made this possible is often enough.

Once we returned to the work in hand, Dr Lofting kindly referred me for one-to-one hourly sessions with a psychiatric nurse based at the Norvic. The first nurse, called Jack, was only a few weeks from retirement. He suggested that I kept a journal.

As I had never even kept a diary, I decided to write down my experience during the previous 18 months from memory. I managed about 20 double-sided pages by hand within 72 hours and found it immensely cathartic. I gave it to Jack to read before our last session.

He found it very enlightening, but warned me that maybe I was trying to move on too quickly, as only 10 months had passed since 'the jump'.

I was then allocated to a young female student psychiatric nurse. My initial reaction was one of dread at having to repeat the whole rigmarole again. However she had read my notes quite thoroughly beforehand and we worked well together. She listened to my fears and hopes on a weekly basis, not always saying much and never giving advice, just pointers now and then.

Although the group therapy had not exactly been my cup of tea (apart from the cups of tea), I did make the acquaintance with a young women named Tina, while chatting over a lunch break. She also found the silence rather tricky at times and became a very good close friend. We stayed in touch after I left the therapy group. I was privileged to visit her many times in the communal area at Norwich YWCA, which allowed very few male visitors, due to the potential threat of physical and emotional abuse. I listened to her open up about her condition and consequent self harm. These were areas of which I was virtually ignorant.

I had to sign on to claim unemployment benefit, soon to be superseded by income support. The appropriate harshly lit office, with the most uncomfortable formica screwed down chairs, was at least thankfully on the ground floor.

I had not gone through this rather demeaning process for nearly a decade. I was, however, assigned a disability officer who initially pointed me in the direction of potential work at the local Remploy factory. It was part of a UK-wide specialist network that found sustainable employment for people with varying disabilities.

I duly attended the interview and was impressed. However for some reason, which I trust wasn't prejudicial, I wanted to find a job where I was in the minority as a person with disabilities, rather than immersed in a team where most employees were disabled.

Looking back I think it was the beginning of me wanting to ensure that people living with both physical and mental issues could be accepted for their skills in all places of work. I learnt in later years that in the real world this was a lot easier said than done.

The UK economy was on the cusp of another slump, so vacancies were scarce. I had attended evening typing classes at the local secondary modern school close to my then marital home in 1982. I could not trace the certificates among the paperwork that I had inherited, so I decided to use some of the divorce money to brush up my qwerty skills at a private college not far from Coslany Street and of course the ubiquitous St Andrew's multi-storey. By now I was able to pass the car park from time to time without pausing, trying to focus on my destination and avoid the shadows of my past. I acquired a portable typewriter to use both in the flat and lug to the college, while using my ever-present stick.

I still have the Pitman's Examinations Institute certificate. I was examined under the supervision of a duly constituted committee and awarded an elementary pass for a copying speed of 25 words a minute.

I was about 15 words per minute adrift of my previous top speed, but I was trying to adopt a learn to walk before you can run frame of mind, especially as the latter still seemed an impossible target. It was especially rewarding to be among a varied group of students of different ages, sharing frustrations and successes, certainly not type cast.

Chapter 18
Confirmation That I Am Loved

1988 was a mixed bag. On the one foot was Mr Angry, frustrated that I did not have a place of my own, a partner or paid employment. I ordered a pair of bright red boots to match my bright red cord trousers, shirt, tie, sweater and even socks.

One morning my pent up frustrations told my slightly addled brain that I should embark on my first long distance cycle ride for about 10 years. Well I had driven all round Norfolk, so why not cycle.

After nearly 20 miles, with only a water bottle to sustain me, I arrived at Swanton Morley totally exhausted. Unable to cycle back, I had to telephone dad from a call box and asked him to collect me and the wheels. This was becoming a bit repetitive and, of course, I dwelt on my 'failure' to complete the return journey, rather than savouring a major achievement.

Rewarding yourself when you are in a depressive state can be at best very difficult and at worst impossible. Even someone else praising you can jar. You start to believe that the person praising you is just offering a sop. Even if it is from a close family member or friend, you doubt their authenticity.

Often I have found that encouragement from a stranger can sometimes be more easily received. Maybe it is because they recognise the person and the achievement at face value, without knowledge of all the recipient's baggage.

One evening driving back from a friend's and passing by the road leading to my previous matrimonial home, I suddenly felt an acute and severe sense of loss that seemed insurmountable. Something snapped and instead of heading home I took the nearest road to the north Norfolk coast. I stopped in a grassy cliff top car park and had a great urge to drive through the protective fence and over the cliff top. Surely I would not survive that. Yet I hesitated, thinking of late night strollers on the beach who might be killed or traumatised.

So I spun the car round and headed along the coast road in a high octane Mr Angry mood and somewhat too fast. Entering the village of East Runton, where me and my brother had spent a few very pleasant childhood holidays, I took a bend too fast, lost control of the car and span over to smash against a low flint wall on the opposite carriageway. Three passers by, a hundred yards away, came to ask if I was OK. It was then that shock set in as I realised if I had arrived a minute earlier I could have caused fatalities.

It was nearly midnight, yet I was coherent enough to go in search of a phone so I could call my parents. I could not remember where the nearest pay phone was, so trudged several hundred yards to the holiday cottage, which our family had jointly shared with the owner decades previously. There was nobody at home.

Upon my return a police car drew up. An officer asked me if I had been drinking. Indeed I had, probably two beers and some spirits at my friends, so when he produced the breathalyzer kit I feared the worse. I was stunned when he announced it was negative.

The officers kindly helped me to manoeuvre the car so that it was safely parked. I could see that it was a write off and would have to be moved to a garage for assessment. I was taken to Cromer police station, the first time I had had to give my details at such an establishment.

At 1am I was allowed to call my poor dad to pick me up. I found out through the insurers that the wall belonged to a Miss Abbs, to whom I sent a cheque to for the cost of repair. So no more driving for a while and I had learned my lesson about drinking and driving.

 I could have been consumed by anger, but despite my continuing inner turmoil, I found that attending services at St Peter Mancroft more regularly began to help my wellbeing.

With fairly constant encouragement from Matthew I even went along to a bible study group at the house of the then curate Derrick Herrick and his wife Vanessa. They had to listen for any crying from their very young children via a bedroom baby intercom, which I found rather endearing.

The six group members ranged from around my age to seventh decade. The discussions were very open-ended, caring and compassionate. Over the weeks I discovered that several of the group had been broken mentally in some way during their journeys of faith and sometimes lack of it. We discussed how this related to the gospel message. I found this very comforting, especially compared to some of the certainties that I had encountered elsewhere.

I was part of this group at various venues for nearly 10 years, with mainly the same members. We always found space to agree, to disagree and to challenge each other as our outlook changed over time. The curate's house was in Recreation Road and maybe this step along my journey was a bit of re-creation.

I also started helping out with what was then called Sunday school alongside Joe, a very amiable leader of many years experience. After the first hymn, we scuttled off up spiral stairs, which I was just about able to negotiate. Mine was more of a s-c-u-t-t-l-e, to the rather exciting room in the tower.

The age range was 6-10. We followed quarterly material from a renowned publisher. I was happy to help with the basics of giving out pre-printed material and equipment, especially as there were no DBS checks then and I wanted to be cautious. However, I did find it rather strange that in a family service, the children all disappeared to three different venues in the church for the main part of the proceedings, only to re-emerge for the final hymn clutching anything they had drawn or written.

In the autumn the vicar, David Sharp, suggested I join an adult confirmation course. I had been christened as a baby, so all was fine with the church regulations. Although many years later I had a rather animated discussion with David concerning the church persuasion, versus the biblical validity of this 'rite of Christian passage', I felt at this juncture that it would be beneficial for me, as well as ticking the right box.

I certainly found the course interesting, as we challenged each other over the weeks. I was duly booked to be confirmed the following February at St Peter Mancroft, along with some teenage confirmees. The church had become a spiritual home for me with several new found friends among the congregation.

I had started going to a prayer group facilitated by Amanda every Tuesday morning in the converted church undercroft. I was the only man in a group of five. Still without any paid employment, I spent a lot of time in two warm venues with free access. I read in the 1960s Norwich Central Library, which had been jointly designed by my father and three other architects and went to the church café called The Octagon due to its design, for their inexpensive hot drinks, cakes and light lunches. I even became a volunteer on the till one day a week, which entitled me to free coffees. It also enabled me to sit near a heater.

Becoming very weary of public transport and relatively expensive taxi rides, I started scouring the motor adverts in the local press for a new car. To my delight, I found a private sale automatic Volvo, within the budget of my ever reducing divorce settlement. Dad drove me to the vendors. It looked rather a sad sight parked in the back garden, having not been driven for months, but it had a valid MOT certificate and road tax.

I was in one of my impulsive periods. It was a nice shade of 'racing' green and at least started. So I paid cash. I should have heeded the very early warning signs when I drove it to the nearest filling station, only a quarter of a mile away, and it stalled three times. Nevertheless I made it back to my parents and at least I had wheels again, albeit not very racing. I did have it serviced at the local garage, but that car was to give me intermittent headaches and wallet seizures over the next few years.

Ten days before I was due to be confirmed I succumbed to a virulent attack of chicken pox. Of course the incubation period is 14-21 days, so that was it for my 'rite of passage'. Even three courses of antibiotics did not rid me of the wretched itchy spots and in the end I was advised to let my system heal without drugs.

Perversely I now became very angry that I could not be confirmed having initially seen it as rather a hoop-jumping exercise. One afternoon I went up into my parent's attic, where lots of memorabilia from my pre-jump life was boxed. In a fit of pique, that lasted over an hour, I ceremoniously ripped up most of the items and filled half a refuse bin. It is an action that I have regretted, sometimes bitterly, over the ensuing years.

There were to be no more confirmations at St Peter Mancroft that calendar year, but David had kindly been trying to find alternatives at local churches. I was somewhat amazed when he called me to say that I could take part in the service at Stoke Holy Cross in March, the parish priest being none other than Reverend David Broome.

I now lurched into a signs and wonders frame of mind, which is not all bad, unless you start reading your destiny into football match results, as Matthew gently reminded me later that year, when I was looking for divine indicators almost daily. Surely this was meant to be, except this time it would be a bishop's hands on my head.

So, recovered from chicken pox, after spending several weeks almost bathed in camomile lotion, I was on a true high only to have my hopes dashed within a fortnight, when the service had to be cancelled due to a lack of confirmees. Where did this put my signs I wondered, more now in resignation than despair.

Initially I was rather disappointed to hear that I would be able to join several others two months hence at the rural church in Barford, about a dozen miles south west of Norwich. However my ambivalence to the venue was turned inside out when David gave me the date, which was the evening of Tuesday, May 16, three years to the day after the suicide attempt.

Of course it was not all plain sailing. David had originally said he would kindly pick me up from my parents' house, but then asked me if I could drive to his vicarage, which was on the road leading out of the city to Barford, to give him time for supper. I rather hesitantly agreed, as my old Volvo was hardly reliable.

Fortunately I made it, despite having to retune my equally unreliable radio mid journey from Radio 4, where an intense discussion on hell was taking place, to Radio Norfolk, which had never sounded sweeter.

Even so we were running late and in his haste David narrowly missed a cyclist on the unclassified road into Barford. I was delighted that Bob and Ann were there in my supporting group. Thus I was duly confirmed by the slightly smaller and lighter hands of Timothy Dudley Smith, Bishop of Thetford. I felt quite emotional, maybe a slight nod to the scenario of Christ cooking Peter breakfast on the beach .

Following the second postponement of the service two months previously, I had started to doubt whether, given the attempt on my own life and recent divorce, that confirmation really was for me.

On impulse I had booked into the Links Hotel at West Runton for the nights of Easter Day and Bank Holiday Monday, with the express intention of seeking advice from a local priest who would not know me.

Lo and behold on Easter Monday lunchtime, I marched up to the rectory, which was near the hotel. The door was answered by Reverend Paul Atkin's teenage children. I told them I would like to talk to their father. He was evidently at a ladies Easter lunch in the church hall, but they seemed certain he would not mind being interrupted.

He did not seem at all phased when I located him amidst a plethora of bonneted ladies. Reverend Atkins simply asked me to wait in the vicarage garden until he could finish his pastoral obligations.

He duly appeared after about half an hour and, over a glass of homemade lemonade, I confided in him about my reservations. I covered my depression, the jump, my divorce, even the last time that I had driven this way, when again suicidal, and had written off my previous car against a flint wall belonging to Miss Abbs.

He replied with a smile on his face that Miss Abbs had been one of the luncheon ladies and, if he had known, he could have introduced me. On a more serious note, he said that I should definitely be confirmed and with all my experiences I would surely be able to help people going through depression. I was relieved with his 'confirmation' but said that I was not emotionally equipped to help yet. Indeed it was not until 2015 that I would finally feel that the time was right.

Chapter 19

Less of a Breakdown, More of a Breakthrough

I had become quite friendly with members of the prayer group including Cherri, a single mum valiantly studying for a degree with the Open University and watching the televised tutorials at an unseemly early or late hour. I visited her flat for very pleasant coffees and chats about our different life struggles.

Cherri called me after one prayer meeting in late May, when I had raised severe concerns about my dwindling finances and lack of paid work. She was very animated, as a friend of her's, who worked for a national motoring service and also attended evensong at St Peter Mancroft, had said that the local office was looking for a telesales operator. She had suggested me.

I duly attended an interview on May 24 and was offered the post on commission only for new members that I signed up. The job started the following Monday and I truly believed and still do that this was an answer to prayer. As with 'miracles', such occurrences should not be treated lightly.

I received excellent training from Megan, who worked in the main sales room. However, I was based on my own in a very small office. The only downside was that it had no windows and I was separated from the main shop area, behind which several other staff booked ferries, issued foreign touring documents and even planned routes for UK travellers using a map and a red pencil crayon.

This was only three decades ago. I sometimes wonder how my generation has kept up with the ever changing technology. I still have my pay slips for 10% commission on sales, totalling £2668-48p from June 12 to October 30, after which I became a salaried member of staff.

I fell into the job like a cyclist to the road; duck to water is not a good analogy given my swimming prowess. The job really raised my confidence. I recently sent an email to Cherri thanking her profusely for helping me get back into employment. It stood me in very good stead for future career changes over the next 30 years or so.

I had been in regular correspondence with John, the nearly always cheerful young man who had been discharged from Mundesley in early 1988, and was living with his parents in a village just outside Bury St Edmunds. I wanted to see him before I started work full-time and we agreed on Friday, May 26 for a pub lunch.

It would be the furthest the old motor had been driven. The car had not been playing up, so I was ever hopeful. Needless to say, all power failed as I was about to take a right turn at a T-junction onto the main road leading into Bury St Edmunds. I simply glided across the road. Mercifully there was no oncoming traffic and, amazingly, I was able to steer into a pub car park opposite.

On the day of my interview I had been told that I would have free breakdown membership from the following Monday. I was now distraught that I would have no cover until then. So, I rang the office and a future colleague very kindly brought the membership forward and alerted the nearest breakdown mechanic to offer roadside assistance, without a recovery option. This was very fair given my preferential treatment. I rang John from the pub phone advising that I would either be late, or paying for a recovery back to Norwich.

The mechanic arrived within 30 minutes and diagnosed that the carburettor was letting in too much air. He did a great makeshift repair with wire and off I went. I was able to spend two very enjoyable hours with a fellow 'Mundeslonian' sampling a very tasty lunch. It also included my first experience of an automatic electronic dart board, whose usage has surely attributed to the decline of mental arithmetic in the young of the last generation.

The car, which another friend of mine had named Betsy, for some random reason, made it back to Norwich. The radio was playing up again. I had wanted to listen to the Liverpool v Arsenal game, which the latter needed to win by a two goal margin, to snatch the title from the firm favourites in the last match of the season.

As I drove past the Maids Head Hotel by the river Wensum, where I had worked as a hotel porter many years ago, the radio sparked into life. I could just hear, but hardly comprehend, the highly animated commentator almost shouting 'well who would believe that the Gunners could take the title in virtually the last kick of the season, the unlikely hero being Micky Thomas'. So there we are, never let it be said that I could not get to Bury St Edmunds and that the underdog would not have their day.

I was still meeting up with Tina at the YWCA on a regular basis, usually after work. Her accommodation was only about 10 minutes walk from my new work place, across Chapelfield Gardens. I could tell I was moving out of depression, as I was starting to appreciate flowers and birds. I was not resentful of people enjoying themselves, but was still quite envious of young couples.

So, I had been confirmed, obtained gainful employment and following a supportive letter from Dr Lofting the previous March had been offered a vacant first floor flat on the council estate of my childhood. I had accepted it after visiting in the dark one evening and simply peered through the letter box. But there was still no permanent relationship on the horizon.

Chapter 20
Resilience to Revelation

Another year but one more full of hope - hopefully. Apart from Christmas lunch at my parents I had spent the previous festive period redecorating the bedroom and recarpeting the hallway of my new accommodation.

I spent hours and hours painting the bedroom ceiling and walls using large and small brushes, creating a white ceiling and sky blue walls. I stood on a stepped stool for a minute or so, until I could not handle the pain any longer, then sat down briefly before repeating the scenario ad nauseam.

Once I had finished I asked dad to come and view the fruits of my labours. He was quite impressed, but on closer inspection pointed out a blue smudge of paint on the ceiling directly above the bedhead - ever the perfectionist.

Perfectionism had percolated into my being from quite an early age. I quite regularly ripped pages out of my high school homework exercise books, after writing only a line or two, because it did not look 'write'.

Although I strove so hard to restore my body and maintain a fruitful life, despite my disabilities, reaching for perfectionism flew mainly out of the window, once I had briefly 'flown' from a substantial height. I did not even mind making a mess in the concrete metaphorically speaking. I did however slightly despair at what I perceived to be the road to perfectionism in some churches, surely not a stairway to heaven?

A few years on, after a service in which I had become much more involved, I was muttering under my breath about perfection. An elderly priest responded ' Be ye perfect as I am'. I walked away and next day consulted an English/Greek New Testament in the reference library. I was very reassured to find that the translation of the words used by Christ in the Sermon on the Mount were given as,

'You are to love as God loves; without impartiality'. The real issue that I still have is letting people down, but that is a whole different issue.

Joe left the Sunday School for personal reasons, leaving me rather bereft. So, I was sent on a diocesan training course led by a rather elderly eccentric, but well-meaning lady called Myrtle Watney, who had years of experience teaching children. I hardly remember anything apart from her pearl of wisdom, 'when dealing with children you have to use a vivid imagination'. That stood me in very good stead for many years. Sometimes the one liners are the best and it is not necessarily the way you tell them.

I was given a full contract at work and had been informed that I would be trained in every aspect of the office, including the insurance side. However the very member of staff, who had helped instigate my appointment and had known of the cause of my injuries, started to talk to my immediate boss about my breakdown and whistle the M*A*S*H theme, 'Suicide is Painless' about the office. I think he might have been a bit jealous at my sales success. In the end I thought I had better come clean with the upper management.

I made an appointment with the area manager and our HR officer and gave a brief résumé of my breakdown and suicide attempt. I was now working in the same room as Cheryl, Megan and Rupert, a new recruit . Obviously they were curious at to why I had gone upstairs for a chat. I gave an even briefer résumé. My colleagues were a bit speechless and Cheryl was very concerned to know that I was basically OK and that I would not try it again. Of course nobody can guarantee this, but I said I was in the best place mentally, if not physically, that I had been for a number of years.

Rupert was very surprised, saying that I did not seem that sort of person, as I regularly cracked jokes. Many suicide attempts, successful or not, are sadly made by 'out of character' people.

Over the next few weeks it became rather obvious to me that I was not being moved around the office to take on other roles apart from membership. I heard a rumour that it was because of my honesty at the recent meeting. I have to say I was incensed for the first time since I could remember.

Although I was not a member, I wrote a long handwritten letter to the relevant union explaining the situation. About a week later the area manager came down clutching the letter with a facial expression akin to Alex Ferguson being refused more injury time.

'You've got a problem Steve,' he blurted out.

'No you have,' I replied, very assertively in hindsight. 'If you deny me progress I will take you to the cleaners at a tribunal.'

My manager then acquiesced to further training. It was the only time in varied careers that I experienced discrimination over my mental health, yet very sadly it is evidently still commonplace in the workplace.

For some reason I sadly lost contact with Mildred. The last letter I received from her was dated May 15, 1987, just after we had managed to meet up for a delightful riverside lunch in Ely. I am not sure if I replied - another one of my regrets. I also received a phone call from Mike's daughter. Her father had died suddenly following another stroke, compounded by heart problems. This was a shock and rather galvanised me to make the most of the rest of my life.

During early 1990 I had a chance meeting with a young ponytailed woman wearing trainers. We chatted a bit as she had noticed mine, trainers that is, not ponytail. She was called Mandy and was a keen runner. We exchanged contact numbers and later met up for a walk around the University of East Anglia lake. However we then drifted apart for several months.

Then one late spring afternoon, feeling acutely bereft of female company, I decided to drive to a platonic friend's home across the city to reconnect. Just as I was motoring down Kett's Hill towards the area of Norwich Cathedral I saw a woman with a ponytail, trudging up the pavement on the other side. I thought I recognised her, so I circled the roundabout at the bottom of the hill and drove back up the other side. I stopped beside Mandy.

She knew where I lived and had decided that she wanted to come and see me. Back at the flat over cups of tea, she explained that she had enjoyed our meet up, liked my friendly smile and wanted to get to know me better. Amazingly she had quite recently moved into a ground floor flat in Coslany Street, which she was busy redecorating.

Mandy owned a small television which I did not. We spent some nice afternoons watching England's progress in the World Cup finals. After a couple of months of meeting up quite regularly, I suggested that she might give up her accommodation, even though the paint had hardly dried, and move in with me. We decided to become engaged, as a sign of commitment, setting a wedding date for the following June.

On the only dry day of an unseasonably wet month, we were married at Churchman House registry office on June 22, 1991, surrounded by the love of many friends and family members.

Mandy stayed overnight at the home of her very good friends Joan and Keith. I slept at the flat, having played snooker against Matthew, who could not believe I was so calm. It was simply because I felt so good about it.

After the ceremony we walked in procession a few hundred yards to St Peter Mancroft Church, where our friend Rev'd Gill Bridges and the resident curate Rev'd Tony Billett officiated at a service to bless the marriage.

We could not have the full service as I was divorced. David Sharp even apologised to us. In the end Tony only changed a very few words from the full marriage service. This did not go unnoticed by the vicar, but it was too late to quibble.

We chose the readings and hymns. Gill gave a lovely address. Matthew, who was best man and me rented very smart suits. Mandy had an off the peg simple white dress which cost about £15 with a new pair of rather uncomfortable heeled shoes, which were discarded on the dance floor at the evening reception. We had nearly 100 guests and arranged a buffet at £4 a head. We asked for money to go on honeymoon on the Dorset coast, as we had all we needed at the flat.

My employer was going through a financial crisis. It was decided to reduce the office staff

considerably and move the handful that were kept on to a smaller unit on an outlying business estate. It was just me and Cheryl, instead of seven staff renewing memberships, booking ferries, selling equipment etc. There were two staff for insurance and a small team coordinating roadside assistance.

We worked eight hour days, sometimes with little break and even booked ferries from home in the evening on a freephone number, so that we could meet our monthly budget targets. My confidence must have been high to work under such pressure. Yet all our efforts were in vain when the organisation closed all the area offices and, as of July 1992, I was signing on again.

I received a reasonable redundancy package and a set of six cut glasses, which went so well with my basic council flat décor. I felt the loss of my colleagues keenly and made sure that I used the glasses regularly, so that somehow they quickly became chipped and unusable.

The only upside was that I had a new consultant, Mr Hugh Phillips, to whom I had instantly warmed, having witnessed his brilliant bedside manner with M and his family in 1986. I had a consultation on April 29 as I needed an operation on my left foot, which had become extremely sore on the 'lateral side'. The procedure was given as an 'anterior fibular osteotomy' and was carried out successfully on September 23.

In the meantime receipt of benefit required attending daily retraining workshops with others who had recently been made redundant. We had to sign in at arrival, after morning break and after lunch and on leaving. It was quite heartbreaking to see middle managers who had sometimes been in charge of a warehouse or small business demeaned to school-like procedures. However camaraderie was good, if somewhat different to Mundesley. There was no gong to announce the breaks.

Mandy was working in a nearby newsagent, her duties included the delivery of papers along side streets close by. It was uplifting to meet up for a chat during my break, even if we were just sitting on a roadside wall.

One good aspect of the courses was the individual allocation of a mentor. Mine was Warren, a very genial young man. For some reason faith came into the conversation during a weekly catch up and I was intrigued to learn that he was a Seventh Day Adventist. We also discussed my experience of workplace prejudice.

Warren gave me some excellent advice, which held me in good stead for the future. There is no need to divulge mental health issues at an interview and indeed, after seven years following a major event, you do not have to include it in any application requesting health issues. It was now six years since the attempt on my life.

I also invested quite a large lump of my redundancy money on some more private secretarial courses and received distinctions for Introduction to Computing and Wordperfect 5. I did not realise at the time that these qualifications would prove invaluable.

I became involved in a newly formed music group at church, either on clarinet, which I was pleased to be playing more regularly again, or vocals. Matthew was on piano and there was also a violinist, a drummer, saxophonist, recorder player and half a dozen other vocalists.

We led a family service once a month, and over nine years helped introduce more than 100 hymns, worship songs and Taizé chants to a mainly very receptive congregation. Initially there was quite a lot of friction with two of the three exceptionally good organists, who might well be involved in such services. I designed some t-shirts for the group members. the lack of shirts and ties proved to be most contentious. At least we did not wear sandals.

By April 1993 our financial resources were dwindling. We had to take Betsy off the road and gave the television to my parents, as we could not afford the road tax or licence. A low point came when we shared a 30 pence cup of tea at the Octagon, not having the money for one each, despite searching the roadside gutters – honestly. We both had bikes so at least there was no need to find bus fares.

Then an unwelcome phone bill arrived on the mat. We were determined to keep the landline as there were no mobiles then. Often after I had gone to bed I kept hearing Mandy relentlessly practising tunes on one of my descant recorders. She was rehearsing to go busking in the city centre to raise the cash required to clear our debt.

She spent several hours each day sitting outside Boots in London Street, a busy pedestrianised thoroughfare. She took an almost life-size fluffy toy dog to sit beside her with a humorous handwritten sign 'Spongy and Boneless'. Her repertoire was somewhat limited as she had only mastered The Skye Boat Song, Greensleeves and Annie's Song. But after three days she had been given enough to pay the £90 bill, with quite a lot to spare.

Even one of the church organists gave £5. We have never been sure whether Kenneth had been trying to encourage her to keep going or stop. I was rather overwhelmed by this act of selfless love, which involved Mandy moving way out of her comfort zone. I still treasure the memory.

My last letter from John at Bury St Edmunds was dated December 14, 1991. He was receiving chemotherapy at Addenbrooks Hospital and said that his legs seemed very tired and lacked energy. I later received a phone call from his father with the very sad news that John had died from complications following an operation. I can still see his beaming smile and hear his chuckle to this day.

By May 1992 I was fast approaching a full year out of work. I then spotted a vacancy for the new role of Customer Services Officer for Suffolk County Council Social Services, advertised in the weekly situations vacant section of the Eastern Daily Press. There were 19 posts spread county-wide. No social services experience was necessary as training would be given to take new referrals from office visitors, by telephone and email, then passing them on to relevant managers.

I duly applied for the job and was somewhat amazed to be offered a two-day interview, which involved presentations in front of management, as well as one-to-one and isometric tests lasting an hour at Tower Street Social Services in central Ipswich.

I thought the two days went very well and the reflected body language at interview seemed positive. Within 48 hours I was immensely relieved to be offered one of two posts at Tower Street. I later learnt from a colleague that there had been 900 applicants.

I have to say that I found my four years working with up to 100 staff either within or linked to the office, the most rewarding part of my work journey. The care of the staff in an exceptionally busy office, with a high level of child protection cases, was very motivating even though it meant a 12-hour day. I cycled to Norwich Railway Station, took the train to Ipswich Station and stil had a half-mile trudge to the office. Then of course the journey was reversed in the early evening.

You never knew what to expect, especially on Friday afternoons. As Geoff one of the community care managers used to muse on occasion, ' What next?'. I also warmed to John, a Geordie child care manager, who had great sense of humour, a passion for football, even though it was Newcastle United and a rather pronounced limp caused by polio. So we had a lot in common.

I must have been getting both mentally and emotionally stronger, as I was regularly dealing with new clients with addictions and mental health issues. However my past did come back to haunt me when I could not help a middle-aged client financially. Towards the end of the interview he stormed past me threatening to throw himself off the Orwell Bridge, which had a rather bigger drop than the average multi-storey. I was somewhat mortified and rushed out into the car park to try to calm him, but he would have none of it.

I brought the issue up with my line manager Joy at our weekly work review a couple of days later. I am not sure if personnel had delved into my medical records. As Warren had advised, I had not mentioned the cause of my disability either in the application or at the interview. Joy simply said that there was nothing I could have done differently, it was not my responsibility and I would have to harden myself somewhat to some incidents, otherwise I would become overwhelmed and unable to function.

A week later, while searching in vain for some gloves at a nearby Littlewoods store, who should I see but the client who had threatened to jump. He was trying to choose a pair of trousers . This made me initially very relieved but then perversely angry. He had threatened to do it and had not attempted the jump. I decided not to confront him and took out a bit of my angst against an innocent shop assistant, who told me gloves were now out of season, as by April the summer stock was in. No wonder online shopping took of.

In the spring of 1993 during a walk on St James' Hill, which runs alongside Kett's Hill and offers a truly inspiring view across the city of Norwich, Mandy and I discussed starting a family and discovered that we had both been considering it . A couple of months later Mandy presented me with a pair of tiny baby socks to let me know we were to become parents.

By late afternoon on March 24, 1994, Mandy was having very frequent labour pains and, following a call to the hospital, we took a taxi to the maternity block at the old Norfolk & Norwich Hospital. This was separated from the wards in which I had spent months in recovery. How exhilarating it was to be back in the grounds for this reason, despite the normal apprehension.

I returned to the ward late evening to support my wife and at just before midnight I witnessed the birth of Jamie Mark Foyster. Mandy managed to hold Jamie for a little while, but was so tired that the midwife passed him to me . I saw Jamie open his eyes to the world and all the burden of future parental responsibility was wiped away, at least until later that day when we took him home.

Our one bedroom first floor flat was hardly ideal for the baby, or negotiating a pram. An application to be rehoused by the council resulted in a letter stating that there would be a four-year wait. We started scouring the estate agent pages in the local press. After a few weeks we discovered a three-bedroom bungalow, within our mortgage reach, located in the village of Dickleburgh on the A140 midway between Norwich and Ipswich.

Mum and dad very kindly gave us the deposit. Although we did not have much in the flat, packing is always difficult with a three-month old baby, as you have to leave so much available until almost the last hours. The removal firm did the rest and Mandy drove Jamie and me to Dickleburgh in the Metro van that her parents had kindly passed to us.

Work was going well and it was less costly for rail fares, although money was still very tight. I cycled to Diss station, but was frequently frustrated, along with fellow sufferers, by late or even cancelled arrivals. Although Norwich is only 17 minutes away, the train was not 'taking the strain'.

Reasons like we do not have a driver, or we cannot get the engine out of the depot, were almost gleefully bellowed through the station tannoy by a diminutive female guard. It tended to be even worse on the journey home and, as the cycle back in the dark was rather hairy, Mandy often had to pick me up with Jamie strapped into the car seat.

Within a year or so, we began thinking of adding to the family and Mandy became pregnant again in early 1996. As we were still somewhat struggling financially and I could see no career ladder, unless I qualified as a social worker, I applied for the vacancy of complaints officer which was at least two tiers above my position. I was delighted to acquire it on a three-month probation period. It meant a considerable increase in salary, which was greatly needed.

On the morning of November 11, I commuted to work as usual. Mandy had a few twinges but given the length of her last labour was not worried. She was booked into West Suffolk Hospital about 25 miles away. However, just after nine o'clock I was telephoned by a neighbour who told me that the labour pains were progressing much more rapidly than anticipated. I asked her to call an ambulance. A colleague drove me to Ipswich station and I was back home within the hour.

The ambulance was there, much to the delight of Jamie, but no midwife. She had been delayed in traffic. I called the village surgery, as the birth seemed imminent. Dr John Leftley arrived very quickly. I was so relieved to see him and asked him what he required. A midwife would be nice was his response, as he had not helped deliver a baby for many years.

Daniel Roy Foyster came into the world at 11am on November 11. I was looking after Jamie in the lounge, but still heard his first cry, which meant that there was no two minutes silence in the Foyster household.

When I had my breakdown, I had become obsessed with the number 11. I even considered attempting suicide at that time. Danny's arrival at that exact time was just as special as his brother's, but in a different way - present joy wiped away past hopeless depression.

Unfortunately for various reasons the complaints officer role fell through and I was seconded back to Tower Street and then Eye social services, dropping back to my previous salary. I decided to look for a job in Norwich, planning to move back to the city as soon as possible to save on the now ridiculously expensive rail fares.

There were not any similar positions at Norfolk Social Services and I did not want to return to Waterstones . A managerial vacancy at SPCK (Society for Promoting Christian Knowledge) bookshop in Norwich caught my eye. Although my reading of Christian books had been very limited thus far, I had been quite involved in the ecumenical Norwich City Centre Churches Together.

I sent off the application first class, 24 hours before the deadline, and within a few days was asked to attend an interview at SPCK head office, based in Holy Trinity Church, Marylebone Street, London.

The interview only lasted an hour, yet I was quite confident that it had gone really well and even raised hopes by telling Mandy that I was fairly sure that I would be offered the job.

Next day, Dora Smith, the area manager who had been an interviewer, along with Peter the bookshop director, offered me the post by telephone. The latter had been rather concerned about my physical abilities, as the shop had two floors and no lift, but Dora had swayed him.

So I started work at the rather quaint old building at 19 Pottergate on September 1, 1997. Our house was put on the market immediately. It took us nearly a year to sell, but September 1, 1998 was one of the most fulfilling days of my life when I drove the family from Dickleburgh to our next dwelling, a three-bedroom house in the village of Horsham St Faith, just to the north of Norwich. We had fallen in love with it on first viewing and even fended off a potential gazumper a week before the move.

So, au revoir to St Peter Mancroft and bonjour to St Mary and St Andrew's parish church, part of which could just be seen from an upstairs window. I felt a tinge of regret. With Canon David Sharp's consent and the backing of Mark Bridgen, a new enthusiastic curate, so much had been explored by the young people at St Peter Mancroft. They wrote a play entitled the Prodigal Daughter which they shared at a family service. I had run youth workshops on disability and even suicide on one occasion.

It was surprising and saddening to hear that two or three of the teenagers had friends who self-harmed and had suicidal thoughts. To this day I feel strongly that honest discussions in high schools might hopefully prevent future tragic fatalities.

I wrote a Christmas play called A Veil of Tears for the Virgin Birth based on family strife. Even David took a part. There were more than 200 at that service. I had suggested to Mark that the children and youth members should lead the whole service by creating a 12-part frieze, four squares across and three layers down depicting God the creator, Jesus as Emmanuel and the Holy Spirit.

After the notices, the congregation was split into 12 groups. The adults worked alongside the younger members to draw and colour their allotted squares, accompanied by worship songs from the music group.

At the end, the squares were joined together on a display board below the organ, between the two sets of entrance doors. David had been rather nervous about this radical approach. Three people walked out. I said, rather audaciously, that it was not too bad a loss. I heard later in the week that the oldest member, 94 year-old George, had told his friend that something was moving in St Peter Mancroft that morning. Hallelujah!

In my first months as the SPCK manager, I relied on the goodwill of regular long-standing customers, the staff and reps to explore the best stock of new and second hand books, gifts, cards, church requisites and cassettes. I broadened the stock so we were not perceived as just middle of the road Anglican and the turnover increased. By 2003 the shop became too crowded at times and the now rickety stairs were a health and safety issue.

After much consideration, I eventually persuaded the higher management to invest heavily in a move to new premises in 2004 at St Michael-at-Plea, a beautiful medieval redundant church on the edge of Norwich city centre. It was my vision to have a resource centre comprising shop and café, while offering events such as book signings. Another book would be required to cover the trials, tribulations and joys of the ensuing 16 years.

So I skip forward to 2008 when, following a 10-month closure, a group of directors including myself enabled the same venue to reopen as Norwich Christian Resource Centre. We ran many excellent events with prominent speakers and authors. During the autumn of 2013, William Armstrong, soon to retire as senior coroner for Norfolk, gave a compelling talk at an evening event when he spoke passionately of his efforts to make railway station staff aware of potential suicides from platforms, as well as displaying The Samaritans contact numbers.

During the three-course supper I sat next to William and, after a short chat, I asked him tentatively if we could join together for a discussion evening on the still rather taboo subject of suicide. He was very keen.

The event titled somewhat ironically, Suicide Isn't Painless, was staged in February 2014 and was attended by nearly 50 people. They were effusive in their thanks for the honesty of my story and the caring empathy of William who emphasised that the term committing suicide should not be used, as this indicates that taking your life is a crime. Indeed it was not until the Suicide Act of 1961 that it was decriminalised. I often wonder if I would have ended up in jail 90 years ago, if I had survived the jump aged 29. It was a perverse law, just the same as saying that alleged witches who floated were guilty and those who drowned were innocent.

One of the attendees was a GP who ran training courses for junior doctors at the relatively new Norfolk & Norwich University Hospital. She was so impressed that she wanted the two of us to jointly lead a seminar on suicide.

I must admit that I was excessively nervous and could not have managed to tell my story relatively coherently, without William sitting beside me. Most of the doctors were very appreciative and one or two even challenging, which was good for me. Lots were sadly worried about litigation from family members who had lost a loved one through suicide and were looking for someone from the medical profession to blame. I stressed, as at ensuing talks to student nurses, that if someone has truly made up their mind to take their own life, nobody can probably prevent them.

It was interesting at the training courses with student nurses that there were usually about five or six males out of a group of 30. But they asked most of the questions. There is still a stigma for men admitting a perceived weakness when they become depressed and suicidal. Also quite a few female nurses admitted to turning to their male counterparts to solve tricky issues on the wards, potentially putting more pressure onto a young man who could already be emotionally vulnerable.

The Christian Resource Centre became something of a hub for hosting events on mental health issues . Some were non-faith based, some included aspects of faith. I was always happy to answer questions on whether my faith helped or hindered my times of depression. Self-harm, listening skills, recovery, learning to love yourself, post-traumatic stress disorder and dementia were all covered during the next few years.

Lady Dannatt, or Pippa as she likes to be called, was in attendance at the Suicide Isn't Painless event. She told me later that the event had led her to champion mental health during her year as High Sheriff of Norfolk, which ended in 2015.

After an interview in September 2016, an article highlighting my suicide attempt and road to recovery appeared in the Eastern Daily Press. Many customers and even fellow bus travellers started reacting in usually positive and often surprising ways.

So, on October 5, I decided to hold an open house event at the now rebranded Revelation Resource Centre, with the strap line, Cry! How to avoid the Void. Avoiding the black void of suicidal thoughts and deep depression had been discussed with therapists at my one-to-one's at both the Norwich Pain Clinic and the local surgery. I told most of my story during the event and fielded all questions. It was quite an emotional, but personally cathartic evening, with a very positive feel.

I had never told either of our sons how and why I had incurred my injuries. Even in their teens, when curious, I said that I had been fooling around on a roof. Once my 'coming out' became public, I became very worried that they might well see my story online before I made them aware.

I told Mandy of my concerns and she found a way of telling them both that was kind and respectful to me, whilst caring and supportive to two young men, learning about their father's suicide attempt for the first time

I was mightily relieved and spoke to both of them who were 21 and 19 at the time. They were amazing in their supportive response, saying that they had even more respect for me, as I had been able to help nurture them during their early years. They acknowledged that I had tried so hard to engage in somewhat limited sporting activities, such as being goalie or bowler in the back garden, and even playing tennis from my wheelchair following an operation. Writing this, the memory of our conversation still touches me greatly.

Due to my connections with Bill Armstrong and Pippa Dannatt I was invited to the opening of Hammerton Court, a new dementia unit in Norwich. I knew very few people, but I started chatting with a trustee of the Norfolk & Suffolk Mental Health Trust. Somehow my recovery following the jump came into the conversation. The trustee was very keen that I tell my story to the board members as past and present service users were often asked for input during the monthly meetings.

I was keen to talk to the trustees, but then started to get the same worries as before the seminar for junior doctors. Mercifully I was put in touch with another trustee and we met up to discuss roughly what I was going to say. She also sat behind me at the meeting, which was very reassuring.

I spoke for about 20 minutes without pause, focussing on the first two chapters of this book. I received an almost rapturous round of applause. One of the board members did comment that he had almost felt guilty at laughing in response to one of the bits of black humour. I assured him that my weird sense of humour helps get me through and that I use it in presentations if I feel it is helpful.

I slightly knew Gary Page, then the chair of Norfolk and Suffolk Foundation Trust, from a previous event at Revelation. He said that with my experience and the way that I presented my recovery, I could surely be helpful to the trust in some way. I was advised that I should contact the manager of the Recovery College at Hellesdon Hospital.

I was intrigued with the concept of such a college when I met up with the manager. It is a safe place where current service users of the mental health trust can choose courses to benefit their journey, leading hopefully to a more fulfilling life while still working with their personal condition. I found this a very exciting model . It was suggested that I train as a peer tutor; someone with lived experience of mental health issues, who could facilitate courses alongside a clinician.

So, I completed An Introduction to Recovery in Norwich and then commuted to venues at Bury St Edmunds for four weekly sessions on Five Ways to Wellbeing, and to King's Lynn for Telling My Story. I wanted to get through the training as soon as possible. I found giving a five-minute presentation about my story to other service users, who often had more traumatic backgrounds to myself, the most challenging. I pulled and pulled an elastic exercise band to its limit before it eventually broke, to illustrate how I felt during my breakdown.

I then had to decide which courses I would support. I chose mindfulness, as I had been referred to an eight-week course at the Norwich Pain Clinic a few years previously. I had been extremely sceptical at the start, but by the second week I was quite interested and by the fourth week I was hooked. I found the breathing exercises and the body scans particularly useful and usually listened to a CD provided at the end of the eighth session.

Living in the moment, when you have experienced deep depression in the past and you might well be fearful of the future, can be very reassuring if you are able to focus on the concept. Even Christ told his followers not to worry about tomorrow as there is plenty enough to consider for today.

I had to help out in Ipswich for the first four-week course, so it was just like old times, except I had noticed that the tannoy operator had now transferred from Diss to Thorpe Station. For the following four years, I worked alongside Lyn, a nurse on the wards of Hellesdon Hospital. We got on well from the start, with a similar dedication to a high level of presentation, making attendees comfortable, inclusion and even the same sense of humour. Who would have thought that. We often presented two courses per term at several Norwich venues until the first lockdown in March 2020, which then prevented face-to-face sessions.

The elastic exercise band anaology had been recommended by Louisa, an exceptionally gifted physiotherapist specialising in neurological issues, who I first visited on a private basis on August 20, 2013. Since then we have explored various exercises, basic yoga and acupuncture. I had been somewhat dubious about acupuncture, but found it very cleansing.

More recently, I decided to try the Rosen Method, which involves physical and verbal 'touch', with the aim of encouraging integration of the body and mind. I was even more sceptical about this therapy, but have found it very useful in releasing both physical stress and mental anxiety.

Thankfully we have shared much laughter along the recovery road which, essentially, is often full of potholes and unhelpful diversions.

Louisa's input was very helpful after I was diagnosed with cervical spondylitis in 2015. This condition can give quite severe pain in the neck and arms, numbness in the hands and severe leg cramps. It has at times affected my ability to cycle, making me feel quite desolate. However I have been given facet joint injections, which can alleviate the neck pain and also lessen the other side effects for at least a year.

Due to face-to-face mindfulness courses being cancelled as a result of Covid-19, I have been involved with facilitating Zoom webinar courses for the Recovery College on Understanding and Managing Anxiety. I have found this very useful.

During the autumn of 2020, I started to suffer from high levels of anxiety and even panic attacks for the first time in my life. They came on during the night and on waking. I was indeed quite anxious about webinars, as the facilitators can be seen and heard, but not the participants, who input using online chat. However, I was put at ease by Mark the clinician who I was working with on the sessions. My interviews on local radio concerning mental health issues also stood me in good stead.

Due to various stressful issues, I was referred for four sessions of much needed resilience counselling at the start of the 2021.

So where does the road lie now?

The journey has often been tortuous, with dark times mentally and emotionally,which have been hard to bear both for myself and those that love me. It is as difficult and sometimes more so, for those close to someone who suffers in any way, as the sufferer.

The virtually constant pain, or at least physical discomfort, caused by arthritis in my right ankle, lower back and more recently hands, combined with side effects of the cervical spondylitis diagnosed in 2015, can cause me to get very low for periods. This creates more stress in my body, which causes more pain.

Such a vicious cycle can in fact be alleviated by getting on my cycle. Rural rides give the mind some much needed escape, whilst releasing endorphins that produce a state of wellbeing. Mandy has been a constant source of support and motivation and somehow we muddle through.

I tried to capture the issues of pain in two of the four poems included at the back of the book. I found it quite easy to formulate poetry whilst commuting to Ipswich in the 1990s, either writing notes on the train or formulating in my brain to put to paper later. I have about 60 and maybe I will put them into a collection at some point.

Despite the trials and tribulations I firmly now believe that there is always hope. The Introduction to Recovery course emphasises the need for hope. A few years ago I was also privileged to be part of and give input to a focus group producing a very simple leaflet entitled 'Message of Hope'. This was placed in surgeries aimed at people with suicidal tendencies, offering encouragement from those who had been to the void, or been bereaved by a friend or family member taking their own life.

I have recently been sharing a weekly video call with two friends exploring a new book on praying with Mother Julian in Lent. I read the shorter version of Revelations of Divine Love whilst on a silent retreat in Hemingford Grey after my confirmation. I have found both solace and challenges from her writings. In times of partial blackness I also turn to episodes of Fawlty Towers especially Communication Problems.

So to quote both the from the sufferings shown by Julian of Norwich and the words of the long-suffering Manuel: All shall be well, and all shall be well and all manner of thing shall be well …Eventually! Amen to that.

Part Four

Poetry

Poems by Steven Foyster

Cry!

I cry when I'm thinking of all that I've lost,
I cry when I think what I've gained,
I weep when I think that You're holding my hand,
I sob when I think of the pain,
If I cried out for all of the times that I've hurt
I'd fill up the cup with the tears,
With anger, the panic, the death and the hope
Frustration, the folly, the fears,
'My God, it's not fair!'
I will shout from the rooftops
'You keep your forgiveness in place!'
I'll curse and I'll rave
I'll spit on your grave
I'll wipe shine Jesus shine off your face!
I cry when I think of the love that I've found
In a church that is not made of stone,
But of friendship and handshakes and twinkle-eyed smiles,
A refuge, a family, a home.
I cry when I think of the joy that I've shared
All the laughter and singing
And when,
I've known that Your spirit has moved me to tears
And prayers have been answered,
Amen
I can feel it quite fair
When I realise Your grace
Can extend to a mortal like me
And Your love so sublime
Healing time after time
From a man who was nailed to a tree

Steven Foyster – February 1992

The Pain

Sometimes, when it's worst
All I want
Is to kick and curse
Which I often do,
I try to think of You
When I'd like to flee for ever and ever
Across the universe, and s-c-r-e-a-m
At precious God
And all my stupid dreams,
I try to cling to You
When I'm tired and hurt so bad
And I cannot understand
The point of it all
The celestial plan,
I wish I could be with You
So I try to keep calm
As I take to my bed
With a lifetime of madness
Inside of my head,
I want You to come to me
As I lie with my sorrow
I cry and I hope
For miraculous healing
To help me to cope
And I think of the Garden
The sweat and the tears
The kiss and the sadness
The pain yet to bear,
The mocking and flogging
A chance never taken
The nails and the anguish
But love not forsaken
So I hold out my hands
As the fear racks my soul
I know that You're wilth me
I feel that I'm whole

Steven Foyster – 14 August 1992

The Real Pain

Tell me how to live with pain,
Again, again, again!
It swirls around like drizzling rain
Infiltrating bone.
Codeine-aspirin-desperate fizz
And paracetas do the biz
Satan thinks it's such a swizz
That potions break the chain.
Lying prone upon the floor
Chant the exorcising law
I really can't take any more!
Leave me quite alone!
Inner karmic preparation
Quiet peaceful meditation
Sprit-guided inspiration
It can be such a bore!
Pump loud sound into my soul
Shock my senses, keep me cool,
Deafen manic moans
Spit the gall into a scream
Let the poison stream and stream
Clear the nightmare into dream
See me play the fool!
I want to sing and run and dance
To jump for joy and take my chance
To leap the ditch without a glance
Have those days really gone?
Seven year's a fair duration
Where's the real emancipation?
Just sod off will you
In God's name
You're such a fucking pain!

Steven Foyster -10 July 1993
For those in chronic pain who are in a dark place.

The Hill

I have travelled this hill
Many, many times
Downs and ups
Ups and downs
At five sat safely
Astride green leatherette saddle
Crossbarred to my father's solid bike
Steering me into a city
Of diecast toys, mugged tea, iced buns
Paying his insurance
When time was not a premium
At seventeen I sped defiantly
On a yellow 5-speed racer
No brakes, one hand, little fear
Life was so real
Lust for it consumed me
Local inns, giggling girls
The next pint to be paid for
Time beyond meaningless
At thirty-three love walked that hill
To enter my life forever
Cleaved to my heart, my very soul
Our tracks converged one frosty Christmas Eve
Cycling in tandem
Celestial magic held us close
Eternity caught in the hour
Now at forty I drive
Two young sons strapped secure
To the crest of the hill
I look beyond
To yearned for day
To take the risk, to feel the force
That such brief life can give us

Steven Foyster – November 1996`

Norfolk and Waveney

£1 from your purchase of this book will be donated to Norfolk and Waveney Mind.

Norfolk and Waveney Mind is a local Mind mental health charity offering an extensive range of mental health services, along with associated training, advice and information.

The charity's ambition is to ensure that no one has to face poor mental health alone and with the right support and resources anybody can create a life that feels meaningful

They offer support services, ranging from personal development courses and suicide bereavement sessions to physical activity and gardening groups. They also provide 1:1 talking therapies, counselling, residential care and access to employment services and provide mental health training and education for businesses, schools and individuals.

Norfolk and Waveney Mind works in local communities to raise awareness and challenge stigma and discrimination. Services support young people aged 14-25, adults and carers affected by mental ill health.

With over one in four people experiencing a mental health problem and 125 people choosing to take their own lives each week in the UK, the need for good quality mental health support, advice and information is vital.

Norfolk and Waveney Mind is an independent charity raising its own funds. It has its own Board of Trustees who are responsible for how the charity is run.

Being local, Mind understands the community and tailors its services in response to what people need most.

To find out more about Norfolk and Waveney Mind's services or to make a donation, please visi **www.norfolkandwaveneymind.org.uk** or call **0300 330 5488**. Reg. Charity No.1118449.

Review

Cry to be Heard!

In this keenly observed memoir, Steven Foyster tells it like it is. Leavened with humour and wry comments, 'Cry to be Heard' charts the first 35 years of Steven's recovery. No 'Shazam-Boom-God-healed-me', then. No. Steven's infectious tale reveals how ordinary, everyday, lived, beneath the radar, lower case faith, hope and love combined to bring healing.

Steven is openly thankful for the loving care he received from healthcare workers, friends, family and church ministers; and equally honest about the people and attitudes that were/are unhelpful. As the story unfolds we track Steven's progress from victim, to survivor and onto wounded healer. At the end, when had I put the book down, I found I had a renewed sense of purpose. Going forward, I so want to be on the side of the angels!

Reverend Richard Woodham

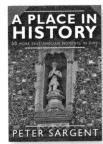
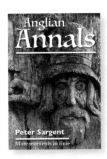
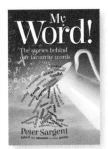

PAUL DICKSON BOOKS
Books by Norfolk writers published in Norwich

Paul Dickson has lived and worked in Norfolk for the past 33 years, initially for the National Trust, then as an independent PR practitioner and latterly as an independent publisher and tour guide.

A meeting with Illuminée Nganemariya in 2006 saw Paul assisting with Miracle in Kigali, Illuminée's story of survival during the Genocide against the Tutsis in Rwanda and subsequent life in Norwich.

After a spell as a director of Norfolk's Tagman Press, Paul decided to branch out on his own in 2016. Since then he has embarked on collaborations with Norfolk writers, Tony Ashman, Janet Collingsworth, Sandra Derry, Steven Foyster, Neil Haverson and Peter Sargent.

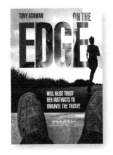

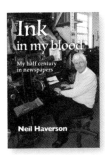
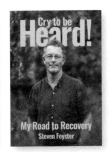

www.pauldicksonbooks.co.uk